Searching for a
Better God

Searching for a Better God

Wade Bradshaw

Authentic

COLORADO SPRINGS · LONDON · HYDERABAD

Authentic Publishing
We welcome your questions and comments.

USA   1820 Jet Stream Drive, Colorado Springs, CO 80921 www.authenticbooks.com
UK   9 Holdom Avenue, Bletchley, Milton Keynes, Bucks, MK1 1QR
       www.authenticmedia.co.uk
India Logos Bhavan, Medchal Road, Jeedimetla Village, Secunderabad 500 055, A.P.

Searching for a Better God
ISBN-13: 978-1-934068-00-7
ISBN-10: 1-934068-00-4

Copyright © 2007 by Wade Bradshaw

10 09 08 07 / 6 5 4 3 2 1

Cover design: projectluz.com
Interior design: Angela Lewis
Editorial team: KJ Larson, Jennifer Maslyn, Kimball McDonald

Printed in the United States of America

Contents

Dedication

To Jerram, despite your appreciation for Jane Austen.

Part I

The Old Story and the New Story

1

Have We Changed the Story?

Part 1

It seems people cannot flourish without hope. As a species, we need to be able to imagine a future that is better than our present, even if our present circumstances are not so bad. When someone truly feels hopeless, he withers. Other things may also be necessary for humans to flourish, but hope is crucial.

This need for hope has long been recognized. The Austrian psychiatrist Victor Frankl founded a school of psychology called "logotherapy," which was inspired by his observations as a prisoner in a Nazi concentration camp. As he watched some of his fellow inmates succumb to the inhuman conditions while others survived, he wondered what made the difference and came to the conclusion that essentially it was hope. Once a prisoner could no longer imagine a better future, he lost the ability to struggle on and he died.

Frankl himself did not think that the source of the hope mattered—it seemed to him that any hope conferred the same advantage. One man might say to himself, "When I get out of here, I'm going to go home and run my grandfather's watch-repair shop in Dresden." Another might tell himself every day, "When I get out of here, I'm going to marry the girl I should have married years ago when I had the chance."

Both the watch-repair shop and the marriage represented better futures and their promise would aid these prisoners to live. It didn't matter if, once they had got out of the camp, they found that Allied bombs had destroyed the shop or that the woman had died in another camp: the hope of a better future had seen both these men through.

Thankfully, few of us struggle to survive in such evil conditions—and yet my experience is that whenever someone loses hope she withers, even when we would judge her circumstances to be perfectly acceptable. Successful people, affluent people, healthy people, children from loving and comfortable homes, once they lose hope, do not flourish. I have come across too many upper middle-class suicides not to take this issue seriously.

Once, a very dear friend of my family killed himself. He was a beautiful man, beautiful in both his body and his behavior. He was creative and athletic. A very attractive woman was deeply in love with him. When my eldest son asked me why he had done it, I told him that our friend must have forgotten something. What I meant was that he had momentarily lost the ability to imagine a better future. He had forgotten his reasons to hope.

Yet, actually, we have to admit that we all do in fact live in a death camp. Everything that is precious to us, everything we know, is in the process of perishing. This is true of watch-repair shops and young women, friends, institutions, and nations. It is true of ourselves. Without exception, everything is dying. Even the stars are slowly exhausting their energy and will one day go out. Of course, it's also true that new islands are forming, new stars are igniting, seeds are falling into fertile earth, things are being discovered and invented—but ultimately none of them are going to last.

The world then is a labor ward as well as a death camp, but the delivery room is still inside the camp's barbed-wire fence. Some people tell me that having a baby changed their lives for the better and helped them to see with new eyes the beauty all around them. Other people tell me they think it's wrong to bring any more children into a world of suffering, decay, and futility. Both have some reason on their side—it is a basic tension of human existence.

Is hope, then, a fiction, no more than a story we have to tell ourselves to make us fit enough to survive? And what do we do once we know that this is the case? Is the fiction still effective when we know that this is all it is?

Some of us cope with this basic tension by refusing to contemplate it. We close our minds to the fact that everything around us is obviously dying. We find various ways to lie to ourselves. The present offers pleasure enough—why spoil it with anxiety about the future? It's a bit like political discussions about pension funds or the environment: we may know that we ought to be concerned, but we find it hard to think of some unhappy distant future, possibly reaping what we have sown, when there is so much to enjoy right now. And it is even harder to be motivated to invest in the future when we have a strong suspicion that nothing we do will make any appreciable difference. To contemplate unavoidable futility leads to despair. How much more sensible not to think about it but enjoy the wine and olives and romance now.

Others of us survive by trying to accept death and decay as natural in addition to being real and inevitable. But because we want to imagine a better future, we learn to tell ourselves that this death and decay is not only a natural situation but also good and beautiful once we have come to see it as it truly is. The death camp, we may tell ourselves, is somehow found within the walls of the labor ward.

However, the universe is not ultimately a wonderful cycle of life, because with each turn of the wheel things grow that much colder and more dim. When the universe takes its last bow there will be no humans left to applaud it, and physical forces are no longer awesome when there is no conscious observer to be awed by them.

Most of us, as a result, are not very concerned about the survival of the universe—a small, personal future is good enough for us to hope in, and then when we are old and full of years, when we are tired of our bodies failing us in various ways, we will no longer need hope; we will become resigned to no longer existing. We burn the fuel of our desires until they run out, and then we welcome the long sleep from which there is no waking and of which there is no knowledge. Presumably it won't be any worse than whatever preceded our births.[1]

I don't think that any of these ways of coping ultimately leads to human flourishing. Sooner or later something happens

---

1. When two of my neighbors died within a week of each other—one a woman of one hundred years who had just received a telegram of congratulations from the British Queen, the other a man of fifty-nine—it was fascinating to observe the different reactions at their funerals.

that forces thoughts of decay upon us. The wheel of life spins but gets nowhere, for there is nowhere else for it to go. Being content with a small, personal future that ignores the fate of the universe is not an ultimate enough solution for humankind. Neither is it sufficient to view death as natural—and even desirable, once our abilities are impaired by age and daily life becomes an ordeal. These are attempts at resigned acceptance of a situation that should anger us. They are like telling one of Frankl's roommates that he is free to move into a nicer barrack if he goes alone and that he won't be mistreated or shot until just before the camp is liberated by the Allies. If we really believe that there is nothing outside of what is visible, we must give up our right to anger about many things. Nothing could be other than it is. Anger at lost opportunities and injustices in this case are irrational. There is no right or point in being angry at our circumstances. However, most of us intuit that being human means refusing the satisfaction of this kind of compromise, and we continue to give in to the temptation to import a transcendence that is alien to our dead-end materialism.

We have to admit that we find ourselves in a very strange place. The very abilities that allow us to dominate the planet we inhabit seem also bound to persuade us that there is little point in our doing so. In the original *Matrix* movie, the sensate program Agent Smith could have learned a few interesting things from Morpheus if "he" had not been so busy torturing him. A growing number of people in the West have come to agree with Agent Smith that humans are the problem. Our "stink" is everywhere. Only we seem to violate the natural patterns of behavior and ecology. And yet only we are conscious of the situation. No matter how much one may prefer other organisms to humans, one has to come back to humans for the hope of a better future. You, dear reader, are both part of the problem and a potential part of the answer—and you didn't ask for any of this. If we were not so used to the situation, I think we would recognize how odd it all is.

In the Christian scriptures there is something that disagrees quite profoundly with Frankl as I understand him—it speaks of "a better hope."[2] The implication is that not all hopes are equally good. But can one imagined future that gives us the will to live really be better than another? Suppose that two men are mowing the lawn under a hot sun: one pictures himself drinking a beer afterwards, the other a Diet Coke. They are expressing a personal preference, but both pictures get them through cutting the grass. How can we say that one is better than the other?

I think that a "better" hope is an imagined future that turns out to be good and true when it becomes an experienced present. When the lawnmowers are put away, the Diet Coke proves to be the better hope if the fridge door opens to reveal lots of Diet Coke and not one can of beer. Many things, I think, can function as hopes for us in our present lives. (All of us, apparently, invest our hope in something, even if we may not find it easy to put into words.) But these hopes must also turn out to be good and true when the future finally arrives—as it must, because a future that never arrives cannot act as a useful hope.

We prefer not to think about death and decay, or tell ourselves that they are things of natural beauty, because there is nothing we can do about them—there is no alternative. It would be too painful to admit that we have a desire greater than the

---

2. Hebrews 7:19.

pleasures of life can meet. Admitting to such a desire could be labeled unhealthy. Why demand that things last when they cannot? Where is the sense in that? And who are we making the demand of anyway?

But what if that thinking is wrong? What if the really *healthy* thing is to be angry at the universality of death and decay? What if the correct way to endure our frustrated universe is to admit that we possess gigantic desires that defy this basic tension?

Many people in the past have had Heaven as their imagined "better future." As a hope, it got them through tough times. It motivated them. It has made them willing to make sacrifices in the present and to be kind to others. It is common to criticize the idea of Heaven as a remote hope that causes people to neglect making the effort to achieve needed changes to present circumstances. However, I find that, when properly understood, Heaven's effect on my life in the present is to cause me to be willing to postpone personal comfort and fulfillment (because these are assured in the future), and so I can better give thought to the needs of others in the present. The idea of Heaven, which can sound like a very selfish notion, has often served to produce the most unselfish people. (Of course, some ideas of Heaven—and ideas of how to gain admittance—have prompted people to become suicide bombers.) But only those who are dead know whether Heaven was a "better" hope in the sense I am using here.

* * *

The first movie I ever saw about neural nets and virtual reality was *Brainwave*. It came out before the film industry really had the technology to create vistas comparable to the ones we can imagine, but the story was fascinating. Two scientists were working together to develop a "net" that recorded every sensation the wearer experienced. If someone else put on the gear and played the tape back, they would experience exactly the same sensations. The scientists worked well together, despite the fact that one was an ardent optimist and the other saw only obstacles from horizon to horizon.

One day while the optimist was wearing the net, she died, and it was several hours before her colleague found her, slumped over the console. After all the distraction of doctors and relatives and a funeral, the pessimist finally found himself back at the laboratory. Gazing at the machine, he realized what an opportunity had been presented to him: he could experience death vicariously and—hopefully—continue to live afterwards.

Being as curious as any good scientist, he opted to take the risk and plunged into the death of his colleague. He was surprised to find that very soon after he "died," other things began to happen. Previously—not being a very good scientist—he had merely assumed that physical death was the end of a human's existence, but now he found himself approaching something bright, like a celestial city, the sight of which filled him with joyful anticipation. At this point, the tape ran out, flapping on its spindle. The pessimist had not yet arrived at the city, but he knew of its existence. Everything he had sensed made him think that it was a good and beautiful place.

Would such an experience make a difference in someone's life? In the movie, it did. Thereafter the pessimist approached everything differently. He was still obviously the same person, but his outlook and his behavior had changed.

I like the story this film tells because it is the story that I think is true: hope is different from bare optimism. Our ground for hope, the story we tell ourselves about a better future, has to engage in some way with what we know. It cannot float above the world's frustration and decay. It cannot ignore pessimism simply because pessimism isn't fun. Equally, however, we should not deny our need for hope because we find that it takes less effort to be pessimistic, and we should not surrender to negativity only because it protects us from disappointment. Fiction cannot be a good hope, and a better hope must prove to be both good and true.

* * *

Many people, of course, don't have a future hope in Heaven. This is understandable. They have never had a vicarious experience of death. Around them they see only decay, and they have concluded that when the tracings of the heart monitors and the brain scanners go flat, then the person the cords are hooked up to is gone forever. Usually they have also concluded that Heaven is a fiction invented to help us cope with the basic tensions of life. And now that it has been revealed as such, they refuse, quite properly, to adopt it as their own imagined future. Sometimes they also think they ought to tell others not to adopt it; sometimes they don't. But in any case I don't find their reaction hard to understand: they don't think that the story about Heaven is true; they don't think that Heaven is real, and so they do not hope in it.

No, the thing I find hard to understand is when someone does believe in Heaven and yet it doesn't produce in him a sense of hope. I talk with people in this situation quite frequently. It used to seem bizarre to me, but I think I am beginning to see how it can be. It's just a small symptom of something much larger.

2

Have We Changed the Story?

Part 2

Many things can function as hopes for us. (All of us, apparently, hope in something, even if we may not find it easy to put into words.) But these hopes must also turn out to be good when the future arrives—it isn't enough that they prove only to be true. This is why someone can believe in the reality of Heaven and yet that belief doesn't cause her to flourish. What if Heaven is real but isn't good?

In the not-too-distant past, anyone who believed in Heaven also believed that it was good, by definition. She might have thought something like this: "Heaven is that good place where God lives with people in peace and joy forever." There are other conceptions of Heaven, but something like this would have been most common in western culture. Even people who didn't believe it was real would have defined it in this way.

Today, we can be put off by such a vision of the future. It raises questions to which we feel we have no satisfying answers.

Eternity has grown rather eerie for many of us. If all our needs are met, will we have no opportunity for creativity? Will we have no tensions or obstacles to overcome? Will there be sports and entertainment—and how can there be without competition or the suspense of an uncertain outcome? Sure, there may be singing, but what will the culture and the language be and who will decide the playlist? What age will I be—and remain, if there is no change and growth? Will there be no rhythms in Heaven, but only one, eternal, perfect moment? I am reminded of the time I flew from Chicago to see a friend in Florida during winter. When I remarked appreciatively that the weather was perfect, he replied: "Exactly. That's the problem: it's *always* perfect."

And most damaging to any hope in Heaven: if not everyone is allowed in and some are excluded—for whatever reason—how can I hope to be satisfied and free of sorrow?

These questions may reveal that we think very poorly about a future world where tears and suffering are absent. Our imaginations are very weak and breathless in the atmosphere of happiness. Like it or not, most of us would probably admit that we find the descriptions of the inferno and Purgatory in literature more interesting than those of the beatific vision. But these suspicions of our eternal tedium are not yet the crucial change in the story that we tell ourselves.

"Heaven is that good place where God lives with people in peace and joy forever."

Even if we grew to accept that our questions about eternity will have better answers than we can currently imagine, how would it affect this picture of the future if God existed but He

wasn't good?[1] This question comes much closer to expressing the
concerns that I hear people around me expressing.

In the film *Contact*, based on a novel by Carl Sagan, there
are two characters who represent two different ways of seeing and
valuing the world. (This is a "worldview movie" if ever there was
one—in fact, it barely escapes the charge of being propaganda.)
One character stands for the scientific vision of the universe, the
other for the religious view. They care for one another, but they
are also pitted against each other.

The scientist is involved in SETI, the Search for Extra-
Terrestrial Intelligence, and for her it is a crusade against bigotry,
fanaticism, ignorance, and the corruption of self-serving bureau-
crats. She places her hopes in the ability of human reason and
effort to discover the truth about the cosmos.

She encounters the other protagonist one dark evening on a
wintry balcony at a cocktail party in Washington, D.C. She cannot resist baiting him about his religious convictions:

> So, what's more likely: an all-powerful, myste-
> rious God created the Universe and then de-
> cided not to give any proof of his existence,
> or that he simply doesn't exist at all, and that
> we created him so that we don't have to feel so
> small?

---

1. There are sound reasons for not capitalizing the word "god"—see N T
Wright's *The New Testament and the People of God*, for example—but I shall
capitalize both "God" and "Heaven" to emphasize the dignity of their reality.
I also capitalize the masculine pronouns when they refer to God to emphasize
the shocking discontinuity between a Creator and a creature.

It's a potent question, and she obviously considers it checkmate. Let's leave aside, however, the issue of whether her confidence in the power of the question is well-founded. She assumes that there is no evidence that God exists, and implies that we may all secretly suspect that this is so but refuse to acknowledge it because of the psychological discomfort it would cause us. She suggests that the best explanation for God is that the vastness of the universe is so overwhelming that we invented the idea to give ourselves some consolation. As long ago as 1841, in his book *The Essence of Christianity*, Ludwig Feuerbach similarly accounted for religion in terms of our psychological needs and responses.

It's a potent question, but it is also an ancient one with a long history. People had hardly started writing down their belief in the gods before others began expressing doubts about their existence. There is nothing new in this—it's an Old Story. We shouldn't use God as our hope if God isn't real. We cannot hope in something we know to be a lie and flourish. We have to think that a story is true for us to use it as our hope for a better future.

Science may not (as the scientific imagination likes to fancy) have disproved the existence of a Creator or dispensed with the need for one, but the claims of materialist philosophy remain a challenge to those who hope in a real and a good god. However, they have not yet actually buried religion. People still find reasons to hope in God, just as others find reasons not to do so.

Consider another movie. In *Devil's Advocate*, it dawns on the audience only slowly that the unnerving character portrayed by Al Pacino, the head of a multinational law firm, is Satan himself. He oozes a constant sexual hunger, but it is not until the end of the film, when everyone's identity is known, that he finally drops his usual aplomb and rants at the human he is trying to seduce with his power. It's a fine piece of acting that leaves one admiring (and a bit worried for) Pacino:

> Let me give you a little inside information about God. God likes to watch. He's a prank-ster. Think about it: he gives man instincts— he gives you this extraordinary gift—and then what does he do? I swear for his own amuse-ment, his own private gag reel, he sets the rules in opposition. It's the goof of all time. Look—but don't touch. Touch—but don't taste. Taste—but don't swallow. And while you're jumping from one foot to the next he's laughing. He's a sadist, an absentee landlord! Worship that? Never!

This is an example of what I call the New Story. This is not the scientific skepticism that doubts God's existence or His role as Creator. Nor is it the old pride of Milton's 17th-century Satan, for whom it was better to rule in Hell than serve in Heaven. The great suspicion here is that God exists but is not worthy of our affection or devotion. He cannot be a source of hope, not be-cause He isn't real, but because He would not be good to know and to live with forever. According to the New Story, hoping in God would be like surviving the concentration camp and finally returning home to wed that young woman, only to find that she was worse than the prison guards. Living with God for eternity would be like a hideous marriage that went on forever without hope of a divorce. There would be no better future we could imagine that would help us to hang on. You couldn't even die your way out of the situation.

I find another strange tension here. On the one hand, if the idea of God meets the psychological needs of our species we begin to suspect that it is too good to be true and we must have invented it for that very purpose. It is as if our insecurities and inadequacies were like a hollow space inside us: into this mold we pour our notions of God, warm and plastic, which then grow solid in the form we have given them. Perhaps this explains why different societies have different gods, because the people we associate with play a big part in shaping that space inside us. Such an idea was already well worn in the second century when the Stoics, the "philosophers of the porch,"

> dared to give out that there is no providence of
> God at all, but maintain that God is only each
> man's conscience.[2]

On the other hand, however, I find that if the idea of God does *not* meet our psychological needs we suspect that He is our enemy. Heaven might be okay after a time but only if God is not always there. We look elsewhere for a better future and we actually hope that God does not exist.

This is why we should not read too much into polls that find a majority of North Americans profess to believe that a personal God lies behind the existence and purpose of the universe. From the look of things, they judge that there is a Creator (whom we call "God)—but, for all we know, these conclusions may be no firmer than a soap bubble drifting over a hot summer

---

2. *Theophilus to Autolychus*, book II, chapter 4.

playground full of toddlers with pointed sticks. I think the New Story is frequently told today, which is another way of saying that, more and more, the people who think that God is real do not think that He is good.

I first, faintly, heard the New Story as I reflected on the early history of Christianity, and I heard it again when I went to a wedding one summer in St. Louis.

3

Why Do We Need
the New Story?

How did Christianity, one among many upstart religions and from the wrong part of the Mediterranean, succeed in sweeping the ancient classical gods away with such comparative ease? It's a question that needs an answer because it is so crucial to the evolution of western civilization, and it needs an answer no matter whether it is a Christian or an atheist or a Muslim doing the history.

Theophilus asked much the same question as early as the second century AD: "And why was the mount which is called Olympus formerly inhabited by the gods, but now lies deserted?"[1]

The answer has several components, but most of them seem to latch onto what I have already suggested is needed for a story to be a "better hope": there has to be reality and there also has to

---

1. *Theophilus to Autolychus*, book II, chapter 3.

be goodness. To forsake one idea of deity for another, you have to be persuaded that the new idea is true—indeed, more true—and it also must be better than the old idea. After much reflection, I have come to the conclusion that this appeal to what is right as well as what is good means that what we call "our minds" and what we call "our hearts" both have to be involved in changing our gods. It isn't a matter only of analysis and reason—it calls into play value judgments and emotions, too.[2]

It wasn't only Christians who felt that the looming extinction of the old gods of Greece and Rome was so unlikely that it demanded an explanation. The pagans, too, wondered what was happening to their ancient, established religion. In his book *City of God*, Augustine tells of one account that was believed in his day. An oracle ascribed the success of Christianity to black magic used by the apostle Peter, but went on to say that the spell he had cast was effective only for 365 years. After that, it foretold, society would return to its senses and worship the old gods once more.

Constantine was the second longest-reigning Roman emperor. His conversion to Christianity in the fourth century was an important factor in the demise of classical paganism. It was not the whole picture, but certainly a part of it, because it was Constantine who made the Christian church legal and safe from persecution. But the *reason* Constantine abandoned the gods of his father was that he thought the Christian God was a better hope. He was convinced that the new deity governed history and was the winner of battles—that is, that this god was the real

---

2. Martha Nussbaum is very helpful in her book *Upheavals of Thought*, where she shows that emotions are "essential elements of human intelligence" rather than something strange and foreign to reason.

one. He thought the new deity would conquer his enemies and safeguard his dynasty. He was not incorrigibly superstitious: he transferred his allegiance and his worship because of a change in how he answered the Old Story's question: Does God exist and, if so, which deity is it that exists? We never find Constantine doubting the existence of a deity, but he changes his mind about which god he thinks is real and active.

As important as the conversion of Constantine undoubtedly was, it is a change in the New Story that interests me more.

My opinion is that Christianity proved itself in many ways and made more sense than paganism at many levels. In particular, pagan believers encountered tensions at the ethical level. For example, a loving Roman mother would not want her young daughter to date one of her gods. It had become obvious to the people of the Empire that they were more moral than their deities, who seemed primitive and capricious in comparison. For evidence of this, you could dip into almost any page of Ovid's huge poem *Metamorphoses*, which he began to write in AD 1. Primarily, it is a long tale of gods changing shape in order to seduce human women.

If I am right, Zeus "died" not because a scientific expedition to the top of Mount Olympus found it deserted but because people saw that he was morally inferior to them and unworthy of their devotion. The God of the Christians, on the other hand, seemed noble and properly austere. This God didn't date anyone at all.[3]

---

3. Also, if I am right, the church now needs to explain the *resurgence* of "paganism" in North America and Europe in the early twenty-first century.

It reminds me of the time as a teenager when I rejected my family's religion and went elsewhere to worship. Such a change is much larger than a matter of cool-headed analysis, and it caused tensions in relationships. My parents worried for me; they felt that they must have failed to give me what I needed. I tried to explain to my father that I had found something I thought better and more real, but for quite some time he continued to assume that the new place where I worshiped must have superior facilities. He could not accept my explanation for my change. He even asked me once if I would return if he built a better basketball court. He had difficulty accepting the idea that his young son hungered to know the real and good God.

Likewise, the changes so many years ago in the Roman Empire caused friction and anger and guilt. It took courage for people to admit to themselves that they had heard a "New Story," a story that said that they were better than their gods. Until the conversion to Christianity of the Emperor, it was an admission that could cost you very dearly. When Christians were persecuted throughout the Empire they were referred to as "atheists." Roman society was perfectly willing to let people add new gods to its list, Jesus of Nazareth included. What angered the culture was that Christians insisted that only Jesus the Christ was real and good. It was not that this denied pluralism but that it defied the accepted traditions. Christians were marked out for suffering because of their innovation. The fourth century was a time of political upheaval, of economic insecurity, of threat from barbarian tribes on their borders. Many pagans argued that the crisis the Mediterranean culture faced was the result of the anger of the old gods against the Christians.

Bear that in mind as you come with me to a recent wedding in St. Louis.

It took place in a big church that was almost full—the bride and groom were popular. I knew the couple well but even if I hadn't, I would have judged that they were very healthy and well adjusted just by looking at the cars in the parking lot and the people in the congregation. The people were very diverse: shiny "muscle cars" and rusty clunkers, people dressed in the bright colors of the Caribbean sitting next to others in the somber gravitas of northern Europe. And obviously they came from all over the socioeconomic spectrum. There were even two pastors officiating, one black and one white.

The black pastor gave the homily, and it was a pretty tame and typical exposition of the biblical roles of a husband and wife. I am so used to such messages that it didn't register with me, but afterwards at the pub my (mostly non-Christian) friends were angry about what they had heard. Both the men and the women were indignant, and I was puzzled by this. Why was I so unaffected by the homily while my friends were incensed by it? It was like the weird situation I had been noticing in cinemas lately, that often I would be crying while everyone else seemed to be laughing, or (just as often) I was the only person laughing while the rest of the audience was silent.

The next week, I asked some bright theological students about my experience in a class I was teaching. The room full of some forty students listened as I set the scene of the wedding ceremony and the homily, and then they batted around some ideas. The buzz continued for a while until they seemed to reach a consensus: what my friends had heard at the wedding was truth—God's truth—and it had touched a raw nerve. My friends didn't want to face up to what the Bible had to say about marriage, and it was this discomfort that disguised itself as anger once they were safely seated in the pub, in the shelter of their own worldview. In other words, my friends secretly knew they were wrong but didn't want to admit it to themselves.

These students, bless their hearts, could not have been further off the mark. My friends did not suspect that they'd encountered a truth they didn't wish to obey. They were perfectly clear that what they had been shown, a vision of marriage endorsed by the Bible, was wrong and worse, it was unjust to both partners. An institution that imposed life-long roles based on gender rather than personal strengths, and one that lacked the safety net of a friendly divorce when either of them ceased to find the relationship fulfilling, sounded to them as bad as slavery. It sounded not only unwise but inhumane. The homily was more like a hate speech. Bringing God into it merely set the Creator up as the authority behind the evil. As Ovid's Daphne felt towards the advances of Apollo, "She hated like a crime the bond of wedlock."

This, then, is the contemporary situation as I see it. The Old Story and the New Story both play around us. Ever since its early days, the Christian Church has encountered both. There have been metaphysical doubts about the existence of the personal God described by the prophets and apostles, and there have been moral doubts about whether that God is good. While most of the institutions and peoples of the West were at least nominally Christian, the Church became more used to encountering the Old Story than the New one. At times, it was possible to forget that there was a New Story at all. It seemed then that all that was in question was the truth of the Bible—if God existed, of course He was good.

At such times when the New Story was forgotten, the Church thought it was obvious that she alone occupied the high moral ground. And she saw her task as calling people out of the darkness and mire of sin up into the light of righteousness. As we observed with the definition of Heaven, there were times when most people would have agreed with this vision of the Church's vocation. In no age, of course, was everyone a Christian, and certainly at no time has everyone wanted to be called up into the light; but people in what we might call "Christendom" knew that if you wanted to be good the Church could tell you how. Of course, she had her hypocrites even in the most religious times—lecherous priests and greedy monks then, just as now she has pedophilic youth pastors and tax-evading televangelists—but even those bad examples knew that in order to be good you had to conform yourself to God's will.

It's important to understand that the New Story has not replaced the old one—both suspicions are at large in the world. People doubt that God is real, and people doubt that God is good. But the two stories can be distinguished, and it's often necessary to do so if we are going to make much headway in talking about our hopes.

The British artist Damien Hurst nicely demonstrated the currency of both stories with a piece entitled *In His Infinite Wisdom*. The carcass of a calf born with six legs is splayed out in a large tank of preservatives, poignantly looking upwards. The object and its title are painfully ambiguous. Does the fact of such deformity represent a reason not to believe in a Creator at all? (That is, the Old Story.) Or do such small tragedies show that we can't trust the Creator to do the right thing? (That is, the New Story.)[4]

The Church, it seems to me, still thinks she is wrestling only with the Old Story, but things go strangely whenever we attempt any public discourse. Much of what we say seems incomprehensible to other people. Our ineffectiveness in the public forum or in dealing with the media confuses us, and we scratch our collective head. We complain that our society is post-literate, addicted to images, and incapable of following an extended argument. We say glibly that it has lost the concept of truth. In other words, when people don't understand us, we assume that the problem is theirs. Like the students I asked about the wedding homily, we try to explain our failure to communicate in terms of the Old Story: "They know the truth but are willfully suppressing it."

I believe that there is far more to the situation than this. The New Story is prominent in the conversations I have with people. They don't believe that the Church and the message she proclaims occupy the high moral ground. Very far from it. Instead, as in the days of the late Roman Empire, people suspect that their culture's familiar old god is smaller than they are. People seriously consider themselves better than the god of the Old Story. Only, this time it is not Zeus but the Christian God who appears not to have kept pace with our moral progress.

---

4. Thanks to my friend Andrew Jones at Grace Church in London for helping me to hear the strains of both stories echoed in the one work.

4

Some Questions in the New Story

Could the real God ever go extinct as a source of human hope?

Gods have gone extinct before now—gods that were well entrenched in a powerful culture and had for a very long time influenced both personal behavior and public policy. So, to be fair, we have to admit the possibility that God could suffer the same fate. Even Jesus once asked, "When the Son of Man comes, will he find faith?"[1]

If the real God were ever to go extinct—not to cease to exist but to be forgotten by humankind as a source of hope—it will be because His morality is too different from our contemporary "common-sense" theology. Think about the places where a rift has opened up between our society and the Christian message.

---

1. Luke 18:8, a reference to his "Second Coming" to Earth.

As you examine them, the questions pour out in a torrent, as if from a broken pipe.

The moral friction between the Bible's message and our current sense of right behavior is not confined to roles within heterosexual marriage (as in the wedding homily in St. Louis) but is felt in most aspects of gender and sexuality. Our culture condemns the God of the Bible as a paternalistic misogynist attempting to perpetuate a tyranny against women. It considers the laws about sex in both Judaism and Christianity hopelessly archaic and repressive, designed to meet the concerns of long-gone societies—and certainly not a recipe for happiness and fulfillment in our day. If God knows so little about what will allow us to flourish in this area of our lives, we can only distrust His understanding of everything else.

Then, the idea of eternal punishment makes God look vindictive. Contemporary common-sense theology would argue that any god who could create something as indefensible as Hell cannot by definition be good, and so we hope He isn't real.

And then any society knows that a well-adjusted person does not demand the exclusive attention of someone else, much less of *everyone* else, and therefore God seems either insecure or egotistical when He demands our worship.

The torrent continues . . . .

Since we don't all believe in the same god as a source of hope, the only fair way to proceed is for the real God to accept mistaken faith and misplaced worship. God ought to recognize that someone is calling to Him for help no matter what name they use in their prayers. Any kind of exclusivity on God's part would be immoral. And yet the God of the Bible expresses hatred for other deities and even describes Himself as "jealous."[2]

The atonement, which lies at the heart of Christian salvation, makes scant sense today. In what court of law would it be right for an innocent man, whatever his secret identity, to suffer the punishment for other, guilty people? Why not just drop the charges? Once in a conversation I heard the atonement referred to as "child abuse." I didn't understand this immediately, so the other person explained: "Sure, the Father kills the Son." A friend told me of another occasion when someone, considering Jesus' crucifixion, exclaimed, "What guilt manipulation! I never asked him to die for me."[3]

Perhaps most basic of all, if God created us for a relationship with Himself, why doesn't He show Himself? Wouldn't that solve most of our problems? In this way, the old and new stories provoke closely related complaints. If God really exists, He is guilty of staying hidden, and so He can't be good. If God is good, He would reveal Himself unmistakably.

In the face of this torrent of questions and accusations, the Christian message sounds "scratchy" and anachronistic. The Church seems to be repeating tired formulas and cherishing a sense of nostalgia for a lost golden era. The gospel tries to make us feel guilty when it's God who has done the most wrong. We are standing at a crossroads like those Mississippi crossroads in the Coen brothers' *O Brother, Where Art Thou?*: identical flat, sun-scorched fields wither to the horizon in every direction, and

---

2. One example is Exodus 20:5.

3. The friend in question was Dick Keyes from the Massachusetts branch of L'Abri Fellowship.

we look for hope and yet find ourselves asking, "Are we better than God?"

Increasingly, we suspect that we are more advanced than the God of the Bible. Our technology manufactures ethical situations that have overtaken Him and the principles He gave us to live by. Who does God think He is, trying to tell me how I am to be? What is the source of His authority?

In the Old Story about truth and reality, the answer to the question, "Who does God think He is?" was simple: "He thinks He's God," and the subject was considered closed. But to someone telling themselves the New Story, "He thinks He's God" is no answer at all. Under the terms of the Old Story, this reaction defies common sense, and seems also to defy the proper rules of language. In the Old Story, we have to accept God as we find Him. We have to ask ourselves, "Who do I think I am, trying to decide for myself what's right?" But the New Story insists that this "self-decision" is where all integrity has to begin. It is this deciding for ourselves that gives us traction to walk. Starting from any other point is like trying to make your way across a smooth-frozen lake: your feet can't find any traction. We have to find something that isn't slippery to get us started, and today many of us think that the only honest grip we can find is in our own selves. Every other starting point would require us to trust someone else and so beg our questions. At least since Descartes, we have grown used to the idea that we must decide for ourselves what is real without having to refer to something outside of us, and now we have become just as convinced that we must decide what is good in the same way.

Christians still try to call people out of the darkness and mire, up onto the well-lit high moral ground, but they make this call to people who are more and more convinced that they are looking *down* on the Christians and their God. When my wife mentioned to the owner of a shop in our village that we teach the Bible, his reaction was wonderfully innocent. He laughed incredulously and asked, "Why would you do that?" What he meant was: "You seem normal, but this shows that you can't be. How could I have been so wrong about you?"

This situation causes a lot of anguish for Christians as they attempt to communicate. There seem to be precious few alternatives.

Some of us insist that the Old Story of truth and reality is the only story to worry about. If we are faithful in telling the truth and the reality of God, nothing more can be asked of us. If the churches empty and their congregations grow gray at the temples, so be it. It isn't our problem, because God does not need our protection. Those of us who think like this are critical of anyone stooping to engage the culture on its own ground. They are motivated by a strong sense of God's absolute sovereignty. You can't subpoena God to a human court and require Him to answer complaints about His nature and behavior, these friends would say. They suspect that any change in language to facilitate debate could lead to heresy and to compromise with the spirit of a godless age. Preach the simple, unadulterated word, in season and out of season—that is the sum of the Church's mission. The message is the mission. Anything else is a distraction.

However, other Christians today are persuaded by the New Story and its suspicion of God's moral inferiority. They think they have to respond, they can't ignore it—and their response is to change the teachings about God. That is, they change their Old Story—they modify what they say is true and real about

God—in order to overcome the ethical tensions they feel. They teach that the God who exists is better than the things we were taught to say about It.[4] We have advanced in our morality, and our teachings about God must keep up with us. (After all, most Christians today would oppose slavery and polygamy, and these are issues on which earlier Christians have improved on the Bible's moral teachings.) John Shelby Spong, the former Episcopal bishop of Newark, is one who takes this position. In his book *Why Christianity Must Change or Die*, he listens to the strong moral suspicions against the God of the Bible and he is persuaded. He believes that God will certainly succumb to the same disease that struck down Zeus:

> In human history no dying concept of God has ever yet been resuscitated. Theism, as a way of conceiving God, has become demonstrably inadequate, and the God of theism not only is dying but is probably not revivable. If the religion of the future depends upon keeping alive the definitions of theism, then the human phenomenon that we call religion will have come to an end.

People who react in this way to the New Story's suspicions hope to save religion by reinventing it. The project seems to many both right and adventurous. Their motives should not be doubted; but it would be less confusing, when the reinvention is radical enough, if we no longer called what emerged

---

4. Gendered language about God is one of the things some people find primitive in our old conceptions of God, and so when writing from this standpoint I shall use neutered pronouns.

"Christianity." Bishop Spong should be free to construct a religion he believes to be adequate and moral, but when it is no longer built on the foundation of the prophets and the apostles, it is no longer Christianity.

This, then, is a time for mutual empathy between those who would call themselves "Christians" and those who would not. To live without the hope of an ultimate and good God is to try to flourish as a human being in a mechanized universe. It calls to mind the situation in Graham Greene's novel *The Power and the Glory*, where an unnamed police lieutenant in Mexico is zealously trying to hunt down the last, unnamed priest in his state. At one level, he is doing this because he is sickened by the greed and hypocrisy of the church and its servants and wants to create a truly human society built on reality. And yet at an even deeper level, highly moral as he is, the lieutenant is empty, "aware in his own heart of a sad and insatiable love." This inward longing gnaws at him because what he thinks is true about the world cannot give meaning to the love he feels and craves; because "he was a mystic, too, and what he had experienced was vacancy—a complete certainty in the existence of a dying, cooling world, of human beings who had evolved from animals for no purpose at all."

Those who believe in God should feel the pain of those who do not, rather than always regarding them as enemies.

On the other hand, those who are persuaded by the New Story, who believe they are morally superior to the God of the Bible, should empathize with those who are still Christians holding on to the teachings they have been given. The Church is learning to live as a minority in the West for the first time in many long centuries. We are not used to facing unblinking apathy. We are used to heated arguments about the truth and reality of God, but it takes time to grasp that the real doubts today are about His goodness. A film like *Fight Club* confuses and terrifies us when the character Tyler Durden (played by Brad Pitt) expresses contempt for both redemption and damnation. And the Church must revise its thinking to comprehend something like the novel *Hannibal*, the sequel to *The Silence of the Lambs*, where the serial killer Hannibal Lector

> had not been bothered by any considerations
> of deity, other than to recognize how his own
> modest predations paled beside those of God,
> who is in irony matchless, and in wanton mal-
> ice beyond measure.

Unspeakable statements are becoming everyday, throwaway observations, and the Church is shocked, slapped in the face, punched in the head, and reeling.

5

Navigating the Stories

When we encounter today's suspicions against God's goodness, some of us refuse to participate in the discussion out of reverence for His dignity. Others of us are persuaded by these suspicions and recognize that God must be reconsidered if religion is to survive as a human phenomenon. These two reactions are two different paths: they don't claim to go to the same place, though they both declare themselves to be the way to be honest in our thinking about God.

It's a difficult situation for anyone who is serious about finding a source of real hope and human flourishing. One thing seems clear: we have no alternative but to be people of our day, confronting this situation. We cannot be people of any other day, even if we watch only classic movies and reruns of black-and-white sitcoms. We are people of our own day even if we don't own a television at all and home-school our children.

There is, however, a third strategy—a little third path that climbs between the easier routes of refusing to listen to the suspicions of our day and of capitulating to the New Story and its persuasive advocates. This third path takes very seriously the moral intuitions of our culture, but at the same time it believes that the God of the Bible is the source of human hope in a "dying, cooling world." It respectfully considers our contemporary common-sense theology, by which I mean those opinions that are so obvious to us all that we rarely examine them. Some of these ideas may prove to be believable only in our immediate, affluent circumstances. And because it is often painful to have what is obvious taken away from us, this third path is not comfortable going.

The third path listens to the morality of the day and questions its common sense, but when contemporary morality itself has a valid question we have to do the hard work of translating the Bible's teachings into something comprehensible to our day. The third path does not modify Christian teachings to fit in with current moral fads, nor, however, does it refuse to interact with the surrounding culture. This hard way is the Christian path to wisdom.

I can say that it is "the Christian path" because I think it imitates the God of the Bible. When humankind was corrupted, God didn't see it merely as a problem for humans. He didn't take the attitude, "You got yourself into this trouble, you can get yourself out of it." Rather, He accepted the problem as His to solve. This reaction of God is the path of *kenosis*[1] and incarnation.

In the same way, if the God of the Bible appears primitive and immoral to our neighbors and no longer a source of hope,

---

1. *Kenosis* is a Greek word meaning "emptying," in the sense that the Christ "emptied himself and took on the form of a servant."

His followers have to regard this situation as *their* problem and act as their neighbors' servants rather than their judges. We are not to say, "You got yourselves into this place of not understanding, you can get yourselves out." Instead, we are to try very hard to make the old teachings comprehensible. This act of translating the truths of the Old Story into language that can be understood by the suspicions of the new one is a kind of *kenosis*, a kind of incarnation.

Christians are meant to get their identity from their union with Christ—this is their source of hope. We are not to get our identity from reacting to the common-sense theology of our day and from disagreeing with our culture's morality. The question,"Who are we as followers of Jesus?" is not best answered, "We're not these other people around us who suspect that God is not good."

However, we are not to be people of our day in the sense that we, too, accept uncritically its common-sense theology. Because our identity is in union with Christ, the answer to the question, "Who are we as followers of Jesus?" is also not, "We're people of the twenty-first century who find the God of the Bible inferior to us." We are not to get our identity by agreeing with our culture's morality and being like everyone else.[2]

Our task is to answer the many suspicions of the New Story, the torrent of questions I have mentioned and others like them. But our task is also to find out where the suspicions and questions are coming from. Is there a common source, a single tear in the broken artery? We must love God and our neighbors enough

---

2. The ideas in these two paragraphs are inspired by the work of my colleague Andrew Fellows, though I have not expressed them as well as he does.

to attempt to answer the objections to God's morality, and it would be wise and loving also to find out where they are hemorrhaging from.

Don't be confused by my map. Two stories, one old and one new. The Old Story emphasizes (and questions) God's truth and reality. The New Story emphasizes (and questions) His goodness. Both have a long history. Two stories—but three paths. One of these doesn't want to listen to the suspicions of the New Story about God's goodness. It has its many reasons for refusing to pay them any attention. Another path is persuaded by the New Story and suspects that the God of the Bible, as we have been told about Him, is not good. This path therefore sees a need to modify the old teachings and bring them into line with what today we think is obviously moral. It has its many reasons for conforming to the world around it.

There is, however, a third path, a way that I have claimed is the Christian way because it follows God's example. On this path one listens to the questions of the New Story and tries to answer them in a way that is most likely to help our neighbors to understand. This path believes that the Christian message still occupies the well-lit, high moral ground, but it tries to understand why so many people today don't see this as possible. It doesn't demand that people in conversation with us acknowledge that we occupy the high ground. And it also looks for the common source of all the suspicions of the New Story.

Two stories, three paths, but really only one human condition: living in a dying, cooling world and in need of a better hope.

6

BOATS and Airplanes

A Brief Digression

Standing in my local movie store one afternoon, I was in despair. They really didn't carry much that appealed to me. Perhaps the fault lay with me. But as I stood there, I overheard a fascinating bit of conversation. Two friends were also looking for something to watch that evening. They were searching on different aisles and so they were speaking loudly enough for me to listen in. The interesting thing was that what they said was so very unremarkable.

One woman mentioned the title of a movie and the other replied that she had seen it before and enjoyed it, and that it was "based on a true story." The store around me grew dim. My despair evaporated, and I marveled instead.

"Based on a true story." BOATS. We all understand what the second woman meant when she said this. We have a working knowledge of what it means for a story to be true. The first woman certainly understood. And yet, on a little deeper reflection, she might not have been able to say exactly and completely what her friend meant, especially if her friend was a postmodern philosopher. But she knew well enough, and it affected her choice. She decided not to rent the movie in question, not because her friend had already seen it but because she didn't want to have to deal with reality that evening. She was seeking some escape and a movie "based on a true story" was a little too real for her.

As we wrestle with contemporary common-sense theology and as we try to answer the question, "Are we better than God?," I feel free to use the words "true" and "real" at this movie store level. It would be difficult to use them in a technical way that would please all my readers, and it would probably take a whole book just to begin to try. But I still maintain that we have a very workable knowledge of what we mean by BOATS. One of the glories of the human species is that we refuse merely to accept what obviously works—we like to ask *why* it works. But one of the tragedies of our species is that when we can't fully answer that question we come to the unhelpful conclusion that perhaps it doesn't work after all.

There is the problem of BOATS, but there is also the problem of "airplanes."

While living in England, I listened regularly to the dear BBC on the radio. It broadcasts in the public interest and, though it answers to the government, the "Beeb" is scrupulously evenhanded in its reporting. What this boils down to in practice is that BBC radio almost invariably follows a formula. The presenter introduces a story and then briefly interviews someone who takes a particular position on an issue it raises. Then, in the public interest—whatever the issue might be—he or she talks to someone who holds the opposite position. Everything is thereby shown to be a matter of perspective. Over time this formula becomes so obvious to the listener that, rather than being grateful that the Beeb is so even-handed, one becomes cynical at its lack of conviction.

Take Airbus, the European consortium that manufactures passenger aircraft. One morning, the BBC was reporting on the near-completion of its new "super-jumbo" jet, the A380, a behemoth that can carry many people a very great distance. The plane was close enough to completion for the company to begin taking orders from airlines.

It was, of course, an extremely expensive machine to design and produce, and it was going to take a lot of orders to recoup that investment. The issues the story presented were numerous—crowded European airspace, the need for new airports, etc.—but the BBC decided to concentrate on the economics, since jobs for British people on the continent are important to the British. A spokesman for Airbus was interviewed, and he declared confidently that yes, there was going to be an enormous demand for the "super-jumbo" and its many wonderful features. It was going to generate lots of jobs and great prosperity.

The formula had to be followed, however. Who would take the opposite line? I should have been able to guess the answer with barely a thought.

On came someone from Boeing, the rival manufacturer that had opted not to make a "super-jumbo" but had stuck with its well-tried 747 Jumbo Jet. And his answers were a mirror image, the perfect opposite. No, without question there was not a significant market for something as unneeded as a "super-jumbo." End of interview.

What is the listener to make of such "news"? The answers given by both men were barely disguised expressions of their company's interests. The message from Airbus was that they fervently hoped they had made a wise decision in committing themselves to the new machine. And the competing message from Boeing was that they wanted everyone to go on flying in aircraft made by them. All this is understandable. It's good business. Both spokesmen knew that their words might have a small influence to bring about the future they hoped for. By insisting on the certain success of the A380, the Airbus spokesman hoped to turn that aspiration into reality, into greater market-share and stock value. By saying that the "super-jumbo" was a mistake, the Boeing spokesman hoped he could help to make it a financial failure.

We can get confused about the aircraft. These two companies do have different points of view, and both are strongly held and reasonably argued. We can come to the conclusion that all stories, because they always involve different perspectives, are a matter of perspective only. Poor Nietzsche came to something like that conclusion.

Our age suspects that all stories are only interpretation and that all interpretation is driven by self-interest. We may decide that no one ever tells the truth about actual reality: all we hear from each other is perspective-laden interpretations dictated by self-interest. We believe the BBC only insofar as we think it has no interests involved in the story. (It is always amusing, therefore, to hear the Beeb when it has to report on itself.)

"There is no God's-eye perspective." This is true only if there is no God who can see.

The "super-jumbo" may be a financial success or it may not be. As yet, this isn't known and it is because it is not yet known from experience that the two company spokesmen could both talk as if their perspective was true. One of the potential futures they forecast is going to be realized. Some day, either Boeing or Airbus may have to admit that what they said on that program was wrong.

As we wrestle with contemporary common-sense theology and the question, "Are we better than God?," of course both you and I have a perspective. No two people stand and look from precisely the same place. This is unavoidable. But if we try to discuss God dispassionately, or "academically," and look for someone without self-interest, we would miss the point. Of course, it can be instructive to read a book about Christianity written by a Muslim, or a book about God written by an atheist. But as we look for a hope that will help us to flourish, each of us has a perspective and each of us has an interest. It could not be otherwise.

I admit the existence of the airplane problem. I have self-interest: I want to find the best hope. I define "the best hope" as the one that works best in my present life and will also prove to be true when its imagined future arrives. If you are wise, you will have a very similar interest. I think I have found such a hope. I want to persuade others that it is true. Yes, of course, if I succeed in doing so it will be good for my book sales, it will make me feel important, and it will reinforce my hope and make it more effective. But I also think that such attempts to persuade others can be unselfish and loving and respectful.

Part II

Three Questions about God

7

Is God Angry?

Part 1

As a young man, the German director Tom Tykwer was given a remarkable opportunity. It came his way because his films were so brilliantly creative and filled with a hope that refused to blink at the chaos of reality. He was asked to make the trilogy of films that had been largely written but still unmade at the death of the Polish director Krzysztof Kieslowski. The trilogy Tykwer was invited to complete was a "divine comedy" on the classic pattern, concerning Hell, Purgatory, and Heaven. However, he opted to film only one of the scripts, the one about Heaven.

Our generation is very concerned about the topic of Hell, but we are not sure how to deal with it. It is the one hopeless idea. About Heaven, Tykwer made a truly fine film which had the audience talking about the nature of hope after the lights came up. But he was probably wise to leave the other two parts of the trilogy alone. Perhaps he was not yet ready for them.

We are right to be concerned about Hell. If we believe that it exists as a place without hope, we must wonder what future it holds out to us and to others. Once, in an after-dinner conversation, a gentle woman sitting next to me said, with a fierce expression and a tone of voice that did not invite disagreement, that she could not believe Christianity was true. I hesitantly asked her why, and she replied, "Because if it is, then my husband is in Hell."

We are right to be concerned about Hell, but not only because of the danger it presents to us and the people we love. We must also come to terms with what it says about the nature and character of the God presented in the Bible. The New Story asks, "What kind of god would create Hell?"

The question is rhetorical, because the New Story has already made up its mind what the answer is. Hell could only be the invention of a cruel god not worthy of our worship, a primitive god whom we have outgrown, an unjust god who is morally beneath us. Contemporary common-sense theology says, "I wouldn't create Hell and so God should not have done so either."

Even someone who has come to the conclusion that the God of the Bible is both real and good must speak of Hell quietly and with tears in their eyes. This is no matter for arrogant bombast or glib self-assurance.

There is, however, one subject that we must grasp before any conception of God's judgment and punishment of people can even begin to seem morally defensible, and that is His anger (or, as earlier generations would have put it, His wrath). Understanding why God might be angry is more fundamental than understanding the nature of His punishments.

When I consider God's anger as a person of my day, I find that three powerful ideas break the surface of my thoughts and emotions. First to emerge is the notion that anger is opposed to love. How can it be said that God loves us if He is angry with us? And how can I love Someone whose anger I fear? Second, the idea of God's anger induces in me a crippling insecurity, because an angry God seems to me irrational and unpredictable and dangerous—like my image of a Joseph Stalin or a Mao Zedong or a Robert Mugabe holding the reins of power—only much worse, because this tyrant's reach is universal. Third, a bigger thought rises up from the depths: doesn't this prove what many people have long claimed, that religion is based on fear and if we remove the fear, we remove the need for religion?

I don't like to think about God's anger because of these issues it raises for me. It troubles and embarrasses me. But when I compare my feelings with the Bible's, I find there is a considerable difference. The Bible is somber on the subject, but it doesn't hesitate to speak about it. If anger is part of God, I need to face this truth. I take the Bible seriously because I don't think I am free to design God as I would like Him to be—if I do, then I *am* actually guilty of inventing something expressly to fulfill my psychological desires. Rather than designing God, we must discover Him, and in this we are in need of revelation. We need God to tell us about Himself because if we merely look at the world around us and its history, we find that He seems to be just as angry with good people as with bad ones. If He isn't, He is going to have to tell us this.

So, is the God of the Bible angry?

The short answer is of course He is. The Bible says so.

The LORD is a jealous and avenging God;
    the LORD takes vengeance and is filled
with wrath.
    The LORD takes vengeance on his foes
    and maintains his wrath against his
enemies.

The LORD is slow to anger and great in power;
    the LORD will not leave the guilty
unpunished.
    His way is in the whirlwind and the
storm,
    and clouds are the dust of his feet.

He rebukes the sea and dries it up;
    he makes all the rivers run dry.
    Bashan and Carmel wither
    and the blossoms of Lebanon fade.

The mountains quake before him
    and the hills melt away.
    The earth trembles at his presence,
    the world and all who live in it.

Who can withstand his indignation?
    Who can endure his fierce anger?
    His wrath is poured out like fire;
    the rocks are shattered before him.

The LORD is good,
    a refuge in times of trouble.
    He cares for those who trust in him,

> but with an overwhelming flood
>> he will make an end of Nineveh;
>> he will pursue his foes into darkness.[1]

Ah, but those who read footnotes may say that this grim passage is found in the Old Testament and is an outburst of the angry old Jewish deity. However, we can't take comfort in making a distinction between the character of God revealed in the first thousand pages of the Bible and what we are told about the Christ in the New Testament.

> Then the kings of the earth, the princes, the generals, the rich, the mighty, and every slave and every free man hid in caves and among the rocks of the mountains. They called to the mountains and the rocks, "Fall on us and hide us from the face of him who sits on the throne and from the wrath of the Lamb! For the great day of their wrath has come, and who can stand?[2]

I was a veterinarian long ago and I can testify to the helpful irony of this passage. I have been chased over fences by many kinds of animals but in all my years of barnyard practice I was never once afraid of a lamb. If a lamb ever was angry, I don't think I would even have noticed it. But in this case, the Lamb of God, who is Christ, is as terrifying in his anger as the God of the Old Testament.

---

1. This passage is found in the Old Testament prophet Nahum 1:2–8 . . .

2. . . . and this in the New Testament book of Revelation 6:15–17.

The short answer is that of course God is angry. We all know that. Or do we? Remember that one response to the New Story's suspicions of God's goodness is to modify our teachings about Him in order to remove the friction felt by our contemporary common-sense theology. And this issue of God's anger is one of the places where this reaction has been most common. Many people refuse to acknowledge that the Bible reveals God as angry, and many of those who believe that it is an accurate revelation of the true God are tempted to gloss over this part of it.

The short answer may be correct, but we don't find it satisfying. We must take that third little path and ask ourselves whether we can grow to understand *why* God is angry and whether we can see that anger is something good.

8

Is God Angry?

Part 2

Part of our problem in knowing how to conceive of an angry God is the bad examples of human anger we have all experienced.

People get angry for bad reasons—a host of fears, frustrated selfishness, hurt pride. Perhaps we can see that in certain situations anger is justified and can be rightly motivated, but very often it is not. And not only is the human anger we are acquainted with often wrongly motivated, it is also often badly acted out. For example, assuming that you are not a pacifist, you may think that a particular war was not wrong—perhaps the British action to recover the Falkland Islands, or the liberation of Kuwait in 1991. Yet even if you think the war justified, you may still judge it wrong for a British or American soldier to shoot or torture a prisoner. Just because his "blood was up" did not make it right to kill or torment someone in his power.

Some of us have suffered cruelly under wrongly motivated anger, and so sometimes we learn to live as if all anger without exception is wrong. Because of the power and the danger and the damage we associate with this emotion and its expression, we may never allow ourselves to get angry, or to show anger, and we refuse to deal honestly with someone else who is angry. This is never a healthy strategy, however, and it has its own unhappy consequences.

We think of angry people we have known, their motives and their actions, and we see God's anger through these examples. It's a natural thing to do—so much of our common-sense theology is colored by this analogy. Think of the language we use about anger: "blind rage," "out of control," "beside themselves." Do we really want almighty God to be described or to behave in any of these ways?

Human anger can obstruct the flow of love both ways—but it doesn't have to, and we can see this in human situations, too. A father can be angry with a much-loved child. A toddler who has been disciplined because she acted as if she was the center of all things is angry with the mother who disciplined her. But in her grief she also turns to her mother for comfort—who more appropriate?—and, still crying, flings herself into her arms.

Another reason why the idea of God's anger may have unhappy associations for us is that we remember an earlier generation's preaching of hellfire and brimstone. As my own mother might say, "We've had enough of that gloomy talk. We need to hear about God's love. It is love that motivates people."

I have to agree in part with these sentiments. An exclusive diet of the wrath of God is not healthy for any church or any culture. Nevertheless, I don't think it is a coincidence that a generation that has lost sense of God's final, unavoidable, and impartial judgment also has a weak grasp on any ultimate meaning to human life and action. Once I did a word association with a group of about thirty students. It wasn't properly scientific—I merely asked them to close their eyes and reflect on the next word I was going to say, and then, in the silence, I said,

"Judgment." The context of the lecture was religious, and so the students were most likely to think of God's judgment. In fact, various words and pictures came into their heads. After some discussion, I asked them to raise their hands if the emotions they associated with the word "Judgment" were negative. It looked as if everyone found it so. But then I asked if the word had any positive associations for anyone, and in the back row a woman's arm slowly went up.

I knew something of her story, and it explained her reaction. She had lived a life of integrity and struggle, but she had been deeply misunderstood by the people around her and had been misjudged as evil by the people she most wanted to love her. As a result, God's judgment was something she longed for, because she hoped that His perfect knowledge would vindicate her. She wanted someone who really knew all the circumstances to come and name what was truly good and what was truly bad, and not just what appeared to be so. She wanted "good" and "bad" to be decided by something other than faulty human perspectives. They needed to be distinguished from each other, and in the tangle of history and the complexity of the human heart only the Creator could tell the difference.

I believe that the first step in making God's anger comprehensible is to agree that it's possible for us to represent God as less angry than He really is. For whatever reason, we sometimes ignore the Bible's clear teaching on this matter. However, we must also agree that we can represent God as *more* angry than He really is.

Wrath is not an attribute of the God of the Bible. He is not angry by nature. He is not eagerly looking for a pretext to vent His anger or for victims to take it out on, like someone coming home from a difficult day at the office and kicking the cat. God is not in a bad mood. Nor is He influenced by hormones. He isn't tired from a sleepless night, isn't hungry. He didn't have an unhappy childhood with an alcoholic parent. This paragraph is not meant to be funny, though it is incongruous to think of these causes of human anger in association with the Creator.

Wrath is not an attribute of God like holiness or love. Instead, it is the reaction God has to evil and wickedness. If there were no evil, God would not be angry. An attribute is much more than a reaction. God's attributes are His essential qualities—how He is, before there is the need to respond to anything. Before the act of creation, when all that existed was God, the Trinity was holy and loving. There was no anger; and, until something existed that was not God, there was not even the potential for anger.

We must ask ourselves if God did not have this reaction to evil, would He be morally perfect? In other words, do we or don't we want God to react to evil? How seriously do we want Him to take it?

Well, that might seem a bit unfair, because when I say *evil*—of course we want God to react to *that*. In fact, much of our complaint is that He doesn't seem to react against evil when we can see it, and He doesn't respond in the way we wish He would. But if I were to say "immorality" rather than "evil," we might be less sure. That sounds like such a prudish, hyper-opinionated thing to be concerned about. And of course we want Him to re-act to the *gigantic* evil perpetrated by the monsters we read about in history, but our common-sense theology thinks it silly and beneath His dignity to react to our own, petty transgressions.

The response we desire from God is His anger. Our longing for Him to make everything right is, in fact, one aspect of what the Bible means when it says we are made in His image. We are told that His anger is impartial and is something we can count on. Circumstances are almost infinitely unpredictable, but God's reaction to evil, of whatever kind and wherever it is encountered, is His anger.

So far, perhaps, so good. An impartial reaction to evil is something we want from God. It's a relief to find that He is angered by some of the things we want Him to condemn. He's on the same side of the issue as we are. This is penultimate language, however, not ultimate. This is next-to-last language. It doesn't get quite to the bottom of everything.

What is it *ultimately* that makes something evil or good? Attempting to answer this is one of the places where our common-sense theology goes most wrong. We are small, limited, finite moral agents and we find that we have to judge good and evil as best we can. We make laws together, but we never completely agree with each other; and we think that this is how it is with God as well. It's another example of the "analogy of being." When we think that God has done something wrong, it is difficult for us not to see things in terms of God breaking a moral law. But when we think like this we are not going quite far enough—and we are certainly not following the biblical line.

At times, the Bible uses penultimate language: God invites us to reason with Him and helps us to understand why His ways are good from our perspective and His judgments acceptable to our sense of justice. The Bible attempts to reassure our consciences. God *does* act like we would in the same situation; the disjunction between the creatures and the Creator is not unbridgeable. However, in the few places where the Bible is pushed to speak in ultimate terms about our moral issues with God, it insists on what I shall call "the rights of the Creator." Briefly, this is His universe and He can do as He wishes with it.

I have never liked that answer. It seems so dismissive of people and their value. It all seems to boil down to power and "might making right."

However, the shock of dealing with the God who exists lies, in part, in realizing that our analogies from human life have their limits. There are things that are true of us that are not true of Him. And there are things true of Him that are not true of us. There is a startling disjunction between the Creator and every-thing in the creation. I make moral judgments—I choose how I am going to respond, but this doesn't mean that I may think of myself as the ultimate arbiter of good and evil. I can be con-fused about what is good. I can desire to do evil. I don't always want everyone else to do as I do. But there is nothing beneath or behind God: He is ultimate. There is no law behind or beneath Him. He acts and reacts according to His nature and character. There is no level of morality more fundamental than His ex-istence. God does not compare Himself with an external code to see if He is complying with it. He cannot do wrong so long as He acts in accord with His own nature and character. He is the source of good, and anything contrary to His will is by definition evil. Anything according to His will is by definition good. This is not true of anyone else: no human, no matter how righteous, can define good and evil by their will and without reference to something else. As creatures, we do not share in the rights of the Creator.

This doesn't mean that God is angered by anything that is other than Himself, or fearful of it. The cause of anger is not our being separate from the Creator. At creation He drew a thick black line. Before this act of creation only He existed, but after the act of creation there were two categories: "God" and "non-God." God was pleased to create things that were other than Him. Yet He remained the standard of what was good even after He created other beings.

The Bible teaches that once the category of "non-God" was created, there also came into being the potential for evil—but this potential did not have to be realized. If God creates us to trust Him and to love each other, this brings with it the potential that we shall not do so. He wants us to actualize this trust and love—to make them real. He does not want our love for each other to remain potential only. God did not have to create non-love and then see which we would choose to actualize, the love or the non-love. Not loving others becomes a potential as soon as there are creatures other than God whom He desires to love each other. The Christian church has long understood that evil is parasitic and has a different sort of reality from good. Really bad things happen, really bad things exist, but they are always a twisting and a perverting of something good.

I am not saddened by the possibility that my wife may some day be unfaithful to me—that is a potentiality that stows away onboard with the reality of her love for me. I am happy and confident in her love and faithfulness. However, I would have a great deal to be sad about if she ever was actually unfaithful. The *possibility* of unfaithfulness is the automatic corollary of the existence of faithfulness. But this is penultimate talk, and what *ultimately* makes faithfulness in marriage good is the nature and character of the God who exists. If we lived in a universe created by a different god, morality in that universe would be different—it would conform to the rights of this other creator. There is no law behind God's nature. There are no rules that He has to keep. Common-sense theology gasps when it begins to sense how things are. We are so used to dealing with equals.

Not being God, however, it is possible for me to think that He is being bad when He does something I don't like and I can't recognize as being actually good. Or when there is evil in the world and He doesn't act against it when I want Him to. Most powerfully, I can come to the conclusion that He is not acting in accord with His own nature and character and is therefore doing wrong. In fact, this is the great lament of many biblical authors: I cannot see, O God, how some things could possibly be according to your will and subject to your nature.

We are, however, allowed to protest and complain:

> Thou art indeed just, Lord, if I contend
> With thee; but, sir, so what I plead is just.[1]

But it can be disconcerting to find that when we truly disagree with God we always lose the argument. He is never wrong, and there is no analogy here. Sometimes we are right when we argue with the bank. Sometimes we are right when we complain against the government. Individuals can be right even when they go against the will of the democratic majority. This is because banks and governments and even general publics are not the ultimate ground for morality. They may decide their own rules and codes of conduct, but they don't construct morality, except in a penultimate sense. God sits in judgment over every set of laws that humans legislate.

---

1. From "Thou art indeed just, Lord, if I contend," Gerard Manley Hopkins..

People try to be moral even when they believe there is no God—remember Graham Greene's police lieutenant—but it is a hopeless task. We can be utilitarian and believe that it's enough to bring about the greatest happiness for the greatest number of people, but this often involves not caring about the happiness of some people. Greene's dutiful, idealistic lieutenant made a deal with the governor of his state that he could take hostages and shoot them until the villagers handed over the priest he was searching for. The lieutenant was a kind man—he even paid a five-peso fine for the priest once—but he was shooting innocent people for what he saw as the greater good. He felt abandoned in his "dying, cooling world" and was trying to be moral without God. He was disappointed with everything—he wanted to shoot all the adults and take the children into the desert to begin again—and this is all motivated by what he thought was love.

Although we are fallible we have to make judgments. It matters which god we worship and obey. There are, after all, many "authorities" claiming to be God. Just because something claims, or is claimed, to be God does not make it good. Only God is good by definition because only He is, in reality, God. He is the ultimate ground of good and the ultimate judge of evil.

9

A Small Digression about Judgment

If you accuse me of doing something wrong (and especially if you catch me in the act), I may well make an excuse. I'll blame someone else or try to show that things are not what they seem. You think I'm guilty, but I'll try to prove that you should find me innocent. And if you find this reaction irritating, you may exclaim, "Stop trying to justify yourself!"

One of the largest words used in the Christian message of reconciliation with God is "justification." In this context, however, it is not a question of us finding an excuse, or showing that we are not as guilty as we look, because in this case we are before a Judge who knows every motive of the heart, no matter how convoluted, and every mitigating circumstance. If we are innocent, we have no need to fear because He will not find us guilty.

However, the Christian message is that we are justified by being credited with someone else's innocence. This is a strange idea.

If the Bible is correct, everyone is going to stand before the judgment of God. This is where the good and the bad in me will be named. This is why my thoughts and actions are not completely meaningless. No one else may know that a person was faithful throughout their obscure life—but God knows the truth. Maybe the whole world runs after a particular celebrity as if they live an admirable life—but God knows the truth. The very same action by different people, or by the same person at different times, may have very different meanings—but this doesn't make "good" and "bad" ultimately relative, because God knows the truth.

Suppose you are listening to a doctor. She is poised to talk to you about the results of your medical tests, and so what she is about to say matters a great deal to you. Different pronouncements on her part may lead to very different futures for you. She turns on a light to show you a series of X-rays. "This," she says, "is an X-ray of a normal, healthy thorax. This is the heart and these are the lungs. And *this*," she goes on, pointing to the image next to it, "is an X-ray of your thorax."

At this moment, you are hoping with all your heart that the two pictures are identical. That result, and really only that result, would be good news. But perhaps there are blotches on your lungs, just a few dark spots that are not in the other X-ray. This is very bad news. She may slide a third picture up, an X-ray of another one of her patients, one in which the lungs are even more covered with lesions, but there is not any comfort to be taken from this comparison. You are not happy or healthy just because there are other people with worse lesions. The only good news for you at that moment would be a picture of your thorax exactly like the healthy one.

This is not unlike how I imagine the judgment of God. It certainly matters to us what He is going to pronounce. First, there is a picture, a kind of moral X-ray, that is the very image of righteousness. This is a normal, healthy picture, the example with which our morality is going to be compared. The picture is of God Himself, because that is the basis on which He judges. It is how He is, or, in older language, it is holiness or perfect righteousness. Next to it is displayed a picture of your heart or mine and its motives and ambitions and actions—everything that we have done with the gift of our consciousness. How do we really expect it to compare with God's? Do we imagine that it will look not just similar but the same? We will find no joy or justification if ours is merely less deformed than someone else's. The picture must be the same as the perfect example, because any difference will earn the impartial anger of the judge. And yet this impossibility, that my moral X-ray will look exactly the same as God's, is what we must be hoping for if we intend to stand before Him on the basis of our own merits and ask only "to get what I deserve."

Of course, the moral X-ray of our hearts does not look anything like God's. The moment we see them side by side we realize how utterly predictable the outcome was, how foolish it was to expect otherwise. A friend who was bitter about his life and his lack of prospects recently told me he looked forward to the judgment of God, because there were some harsh things he planned to say to Him. But this is courting catastrophe. I subsequently received a letter from the same friend, who is now doing time in prison, and he admitted how stupid his attitude had been. It was so important that he got this straight, and I was happy that he had reconsidered his position.

However, God has, as it were, a third X-ray, and the Christian message is that this picture may be attributed to us. We can be justified. This image belongs to Jesus, and it is exactly the same as God's. Jesus was innocent: he always obeyed God's will, he resisted every temptation, he was identical to God in his moral character—and yet he had weathered all the ravages of human existence. This is the *kenosis*. This is the incarnation. It contains a great many mysteries, but it also begins to make a great deal of moral sense. The New Testament's largest concept for salvation is "union with the Christ." We are united with him in his death and resurrection and the Old Testament says of the Messiah that "by his wounds we are healed."[1] My hope rests not in my own innocence but in the perfection of the sacrifice with which I am united.

We long for our lives and our actions to have significance. We don't want to believe that suffering for good is the same as suffering for evil, and we don't want suffering to be the same as not suffering at all. And significance is precisely what we have been given: it matters what we do. Our significance flows from the God who created us, knows us, and will judge us. Our hope for significance flows back to us from the future judgment of God. If He loved us without regard for what we do, it would rob us of that gift of significance.

But the Christian message offers this additional hope: that though we are condemned by the very significance we long for and have misused, there is yet a means to escape God's anger. Rather than seeking to stand before Him on our own merits,

---

1. Isaiah 53:5.

we can meet Him in His mercy, credited with an innocence that does not belong to us.

God is the ground of good, the source of meaning and significance, and our only hope of innocence and eternal happiness.

10

Is God Distant?

Part 1

When I was a child, my family would often go to church in two cars. My father was a successful attorney and right after the service he would go to the airport to catch a plane while the rest of us would drive home. He would return on Thursday night after I had gone to bed. I realize now that while he was away he was working hard somewhere, preparing for a big trial. This was how he could afford to pay for my private schooling, my trips abroad and, later, my little convertible sports cars.

My father was a child of the Depression in the early part of the twentieth century and he had grown up in poverty. Being able to provide for his family was therefore a very high priority for him, and he was good at it. I was a child and I wanted all the toys that his success brought to me, and so it would be very unfair of me now to complain that what I *really* wanted all those years, much more than the shiny stuff, was a close relationship with my dad. And yet there's a lot of truth in that complaint made in the hindsight of my adulthood.

My father was not a deadbeat who refused to pay alimony or child-support. I never once had the thought that he might abandon my mother or me. He was a good man who did his duty before anything else. Nevertheless, my memories are more of his absence than his presence.

Many of us feel something like this when we think about God.

We want a hope for the future and we want a sense of belonging in the present. The New Story that doubts God's goodness acknowledges our emotional needs and the fact that they are apparently woven into the fabric of our humanity, and it accuses God of having let us down like a too-busy parent who should have known better. You cannot expect the child to make a wise choice: it is the parent who must take responsibility for the relational needs of the family.

Feeling abandoned by our parents can make us very angry, and the greater our desire for intimacy and security the deeper our disappointment and anger. These can manifest themselves in a pretended apathy, or they can provoke us to try to break the other person's heart in return. It's not a pretty picture. In a very similar way, some of us are angry with God. He promised a great deal but He hasn't delivered. And it wasn't wealth that we wanted but His love and comfort. He has been more absent than present. People shouldn't have children if they're not going to be good parents, and a god shouldn't create people if he's going to leave them on their own in a latch-key universe. No wonder some of us couldn't care less about religion. No wonder some of us raise self-destructive hell.

How can we believe that God is good when we know He has left us alone?

I find it fascinating that one of the stories Jesus told seems to echo some of our suspicions:

> A man planted a vineyard, rented it to some
> farmers and went away for a long time . . . .[1]

In this parable, the planter of the vineyard represents the Creator. Jesus doesn't deny that God can seem like a long-absent landlord. Our perception of His hiddenness is not wholly unreasonable. That, however, is only the first line and the context of the story:

> A man planted a vineyard, rented it to some
> farmers and went away for a long time. At har-
> vest time he sent a servant to the tenants so
> they would give him some of the fruit of the
> vineyard. But the tenants beat him and sent
> him away empty-handed.

Not all times are the same, and we are not very good judges of where we are in time. There is a harvest different from the growing season, but we are a people for the most part distant from the land and its seasons. We have grown used to having grapefruit for breakfast in February, and the patient allegories of an agricultural day may not resonate with us. The shocking thing in this story, however, is that for some reason the tenants have decided that they owe the owner of the vineyard nothing.

---

1. This wording comes from Luke 20:9–18, but the parable is found also in Matthew and Mark.

He does maintain contact with them, and so, however much they may insist on it, the tenants cannot proclaim themselves innocent and abandoned victims. Their behavior betrays them and the secret workings of their hearts. Thinking the owner has gone far away and for a long time, they show aspects of their character we might not have suspected existed if we knew them only under the eye of their landlord.

> He sent another servant, but that one also they beat and treated shamefully and sent away empty-handed. He sent still a third, and they wounded him and threw him out.

By this point, it would be absurd for the tenants to complain about an "absentee landlord." If they had any regard for the owner, they would treat his representatives with respect, hanging on their every word, eager to send a good report back to the man to whom they owe so much. And how is it that these tenants know the man so well? The story hints that, though the landlord is far away, it is possible nonetheless to know his mind and will.

> Then the owner of the vineyard said, "What shall I do? I will send my son, whom I love; perhaps they will respect him."

The man is being patient. In this story there is no reason to believe that he wants the dispute to end badly. He makes contact through the most intimate of representatives. If anything, his optimism seems a bit naive, because we are certainly beginning to get a sense of what he can expect from these men.

> But when the tenants saw him, they talked the
> matter over. "This is the heir," they said. "Let's
> kill him, and the inheritance will be ours." So
> they threw him out of the vineyard and killed
> him.

It is not a pleasant story. Jesus is foretelling what his own
fate will be, of course—having come from the landlord as his
son, speaking only the words given to him by his father, reveal-
ing the character of the landlord perfectly. In this case, if you
loved the landlord, you would also love his messenger.

Then Jesus asks a provocative question:

> What then will the owner of the vineyard do
> to them?

Is this a question allowed by our common-sense theology?
Are people going to be held responsible for their behavior when
they think no one's watching? Or are we going to blame the
landlord? It's a difficult issue. We know that children should behave when their parents are out for the evening, but we also
know that children under a certain age shouldn't be left alone
in the first place. I suppose that what makes the difference is
whether the children in question know what's right and what's
expected of them and are capable of doing it.

Jesus' parables have their limitations—no single story can
show an issue from every perspective. They are only illustrations.
This one uses a commercial relationship as its example; in other
instances Jesus used other kinds of relationships for the set-up of
the story. However, in this case Jesus answers his own question
with surprising firmness:

"He will come and kill those tenants and give
the vineyard to others."

When the people heard this, they said, "May
this never be!"

Jesus looked directly at them and asked,
"Then what is the meaning of that which is
written:

"The stone the builders rejected
    has become the capstone"?

Everyone who falls on that stone will be
broken to pieces, but he on whom it falls will
be crushed."

Perhaps we agree with Jesus' audience—may this never be!
There is no need for God to go elsewhere to find faithful chil-
dren. Here we are. We mean well and we long for His love and
for His will to be done. We want to give Him everything we owe
Him as our Creator. We have listened carefully to the messengers
He sent us.

Yet the story tells us that some of us use God's distance as
an opportunity for evil. And, besides implying that He has representatives who know Him and His wishes, it also suggests that
if some of us are faithless, He can begin new relationships with
others who are more deserving of His benefits, more willing to
listen. If we wish to complain of God's distance, we must be willing to stand up to a very thorough scrutiny ourselves.

Thus, the Bible's first answer to our question is, "Yes, God is
distant—but we have not been left alone." This is, however, only
its first answer.

11

Is God Distant?

Part 2

A few years ago, the *Economist* reported the results of a study that should cause us all to examine our memories. Researchers had monitored a large group of people over many years. They asked them as young adolescents if they had had a happy childhood, and then they asked them the same question decades later in middle age. The point of such a study is to help counselors, for example, to understand how to interpret people's perspectives on their own backgrounds. The issue is not what actually happened to them as children but their recollection and interpretation of what happened and how these evaluations change over time. This is useful stuff to know.

The results, however, were strange and counter-intuitive. There was no pattern discernible in the data from which one could predict who was going to say what about their past. Whether people remembered their childhood as happy or unhappy in early adolescence seemed to have no obvious bearing on how they saw it in middle age. One would expect that the story we tell ourselves early on about our background would deeply color our later experience. It's disconcerting that any re-evaluation in this important history I tell myself is as likely as any other. If I'm not the expert on my history, who is?

God is distant, an absentee landlord gone on a long journey, though we haven't been left alone. However, the Bible has more to say about the hiddenness of God, and for our generation it is as counter-intuitive as the idea that we may not be best qualified to tell our own stories.

> The wrath of God is being revealed from heaven against all the godlessness and wickedness of men who suppress the truth by their wickedness, since what may be known about God is plain to them, because God has made it plain to them. For since the creation of the world, God's invisible qualities—his eternal power and divine nature—have been clearly seen, being understood from what has been made, so that men are without excuse.
>
> For although they knew God, they neither glorified him as God nor gave thanks to him, but their thinking became futile and their foolish hearts were darkened. Although they claimed to be wise, they became fools.[1]

---

1. Romans 1:18–22. The story of Jesus, his character, and his teachings in some ways speak for themselves and proclaim their own value. But his apostles also had the task of explaining the Christ's life in the context of both Jewish history and the future of the universal Church. This is so much the case with Paul that some people today want to say that he "invented Christianity," as if

This mouthful is very offensive to the New Story. It agrees that we and God are alienated and distant from each other, but it insists that the real story is that it is we who have created the distance. This would simply not be an acceptable opinion to air on a talk show discussing the ills of the world.

The passage is dense with meaning, but let me mention just two of the points I find most intriguing—two things that over time I've come to see as profoundly true. The first is this idea that we suppress the truth. The second is the crucial role that gratitude plays in our lives.

How is the truth suppressed? I can suppress the truth myself, but when I do I rarely admit it, even to myself. There are many reasons why I may not want to see clearly and prefer self-deception. For example, I may consider it to my advantage not to know that something is the case because ignorance allows me the freedom to act as I wish and at the same time to feel good about myself and my behavior. Over time, this cultivated ignorance can become ingrained and I can lose the ability to see that I have created my own fantasy. The true story might expose my desires as a selfishness I don't want to acknowledge. It might hurt my feelings, make me see things in myself I don't want to admit. Therefore, I suppress it.

One of the themes of the David Mamet film *House of Games* is deception. A very honest female psychologist becomes embroiled with a group of con-men on the wet streets of a city at night. She begins to study them, because she wants to understand the motives of the human heart. She wants to be able

---

he took it in a direction Jesus had not intended. However, this has not been the understanding of the Church since very, very early in its history.

to help them give up their compulsions. It's a fine little movie, containing lots of plot twists, like any good film about con-men. However, as we watch the plot develop it dawns on us that the psychologist's research is just a story she has invented to keep the truth about herself from herself. Her honesty itself is a sham. She is attracted by people who have decided to ignore the usual rules of society and prey on the psychology of others. She wants to look respectable and moral and in control in her well-lit office, but at night she wants to break all the rules herself.

Woody Allen, when asked to explain some of his behavior that was currently scandalizing the public (to its delight), was honest enough to reply, "The heart wants what it wants."

But a true story can be suppressed in other ways, too. I am not alone, locked up in my own ego, with only my opinions and desires. Other people can suppress the true story for me.

If my little daughter was taking a walk down the street with my wife, she might see a big chestnut tree and ask, "Who made that?" It's a big question, and worthy of childhood, as the best questions are. And Chryse might answer, as many an evolutionary biologist would, no doubt, "Nobody made it—though I know it looks like somebody must have."

This book is trying to wrestle with the New Story, and a response to this answer, or to materialist biology, would be the task of a book that dealt with the Old Story. Here I want only to show how a true story can be suppressed. The point is that my wife's words could strongly influence our daughter's future. She would be telling her the story of a dying, cooling world with nothing outside it in which to hope. If her answer was wrong, she would have helped to suppress the truth. (Then again, if there is no Creator, the stories my daughter hears at Sunday school are suppressing the truth and are brain-washing her just as one of my neighbors insists they are.)

Once I spoke with a group of scientists from the Chinese space program. They were amazed by my remarks about an open universe in which a Creator might still intervene. It was not what I said that astonished them so much as it was me saying it—as if I was one of those huge computer-generated dinosaurs in *Jurassic Park*. They had never knowingly met an educated person who believed such a thing. That story had been suppressed for them by all their institutions. One of them exclaimed, quite rightly, "But this would change everything!"

Life is complicated. My daughter might ask, "Who made that tree?" and her mother, believing that the universe does not exist of itself, might answer, "God did"—and any passing Christian might be tempted to think that this answer does not suppress the truth. But that would be to make a crucial mistake. Much of the power behind the New Story's suspicions arises at precisely this point. It would be possible for Chryse to say that God made the tree and then go on to deny the truth of her words by living a life devoid of joy and gratitude and beauty. An orthodox response in words alone does not guarantee that the truth is being expressed fully. Non-believers look at the lives of those who claim to know God and His ways and they are not impressed—and they have a strong intuition[2] that someone who really knew a good God and His ways would be very impressive, not just in their words but in their life.

---

2. I borrow some of my meaning of "a strong intuition" from Charles Taylor's *Sources of the Self*.

The New Story is right to expect that gratitude should characterize people who are in contact with God. The passage from Romans quoted above agrees with this moral intuition. If we don't believe that God exists, or that the God who exists is good, we will not have a grateful heart. But does that matter? My father worked very hard to provide for me; it was the principal reason for his absence, and I wasn't particularly thankful. Did that matter?

In the twenty-first century, now that we know a good deal about weather patterns and chaos theory, it feels awkwardly dated if we give thanks for rain. Knowing a good deal about horticulture, we may be mildly embarrassed at a church's harvest festival. Today's educated neo-pagan may not think there is anyone to thank for the rain and the harvest, so they feel grateful to the earth itself, because they have found that people don't flourish unless they are grateful. We are haunted by the need to be thankful. If we don't thank the Creator, the old idols begin re-emerging from the darkness, despite all our technology and our university degrees.

Italo Calvino was an Italian author whose parents were both botanists, and though they sent him to a Catholic school they forbade him to attend daily chapel. Being the only one in his circle of friends who didn't go must have had some interesting effects on the child, and yet as an adult Calvino wrote beautifully about the haunted world we inhabit. In his short story *The Enchanted Garden*, a boy and a girl are wandering about:

> Everything was so beautiful: narrow turnings
> and high, curling eucalyptus leaves and patch
> es of sky; but there was always the worrying
> thought that it was not their garden, and that

they might be chased away at any moment. But
not a sound could be heard. A flight of chat-
tering sparrows rose from a clump of arbutus
at a turn in the path. Then all was silent again.
Perhaps it was an abandoned garden?

In their exploration, they come upon a swim-
ming pool:

They crept up to the edge: it was lined with blue
tiles and filled to the brim with clear water. How
lovely it would be to bathe in! "Shall we have
a dip?" Giovannino asked Serenella. The idea
must have been quite dangerous if he asked her
instead of just saying "In we go!" But the water was clear and blue, and Serenella was never
frightened. She jumped off the wheelbarrow
and put her bunch of flowers in it. They were
already in their bathing dresses, as they'd been
out hunting crabs till just before. Giovannino
plunged in; not from the diving board, as the
splash would have made too much noise, but
from the edge of the pool. Down and down
he went with his eyes wide open, seeing only
the blue from the tiles and his pink hands like
goldfish; it was not the same as under the sea,
full of shapeless green-black shadows. A pink
form appeared above him: Serenella!

He took her hand and they swam up to the
surface, rather anxiously. No, there was no one
watching them at all. But it was not so nice

as they'd thought it would be, they always had
that uncomfortable feeling that they had no
right to any of this, and might be chased out
at any moment. . . . Perhaps it was the fear of a
spell which hung over this villa and garden and
over all these lovely, comfortable things, like
some ancient injustice committed long ago.

Most of us continue to teach our children to say "thank
you"—though middle-aged people always seem to remember
that children were more grateful in the past than they are now.
If we have lived abroad, we may have learned that different cultures show gratitude in different ways. Living in Nepal, it took
me quite some time to realize that people didn't use any words
to express their thanks but "said" it with their eyes. Yet the fact
that ways of showing gratitude vary between cultures—and
families and generations—doesn't mean that gratitude is something wholly constructed by culture. I would maintain that a
culture that encourages gratitude is better than one that has no
place for gratitude in any form (though I doubt that such a culture exists). This "better" is ultimately grounded in the existence
of a God who approves of gratitude and who has put a need for
it in our hearts.

There are other obstacles to gratitude besides the Old Story's
suspicions that no one is watching us take a dip in the swim-
ming pool and that socio-biology promises to find a genetic explanation for our urge to thank someone. It is difficult to be
thankful when we see or experience so much suffering and evil,
when everything is not so beautiful and the water is not always
clear and blue. As the Devil said to God about Job, "Of course
he loves you. Look at all you've done for him! But let me strip

him of your blessings and you'll find that he loves you for your gifts and not for yourself."

In the Christian account of our world, however, it is wrong to see no cause for joy and gratitude; and yet in that same story —because it is as complex as reality—it is also wrong to prevent someone from lamenting. Our lives are not only goodness, but they are also not only suffering. It can be difficult to explain the existence of evil, but it's also hard to account for the existence of good when you think about it—and the fact that we are surprised by the existence of either may be hardest of all to explain.

When I am not grateful, a distance begins to appear between me and the source of the good. I become alienated from people as well as from God when I move straight on from one satisfied desire to the next one as yet unfulfilled without pausing to say thank you—and it is me that is creating the distance. This is why we don't let our children tear open all their Christmas presents as quickly as they want to, but instead make them read the cards on the outside of the wrapping paper.

I find that it isn't just my circumstances that obstruct my thankfulness. I, too, am a part of the dynamic. I am haunted by the need to give thanks, but I also don't want to thank anyone other than myself. I think I deserve good things because I want them and am at the center of everything. I think I have achieved the good things I experience by my own efforts and cleverness. I'm afraid to be grateful to someone else because that would make me smaller and give someone else leverage in my life.

Honesty makes me reflect that I don't deserve all the good I experience (just as I don't deserve all the suffering that comes my way). And in honesty I must admit that I haven't caused all the good I experience by my own efforts.

Another reason I find I am not grateful is that nothing I acquire perfectly satisfies my cravings—any blessing I have received could be improved on. My spouse could be better, my career could be better, my children could be better. I am dissatisfied. I'm afraid that if I am grateful I may lose control of my desires—after all, who else can I rely on to look out for my fulfillment? I don't want to recognize someone else's generosity, because that would be to admit that I'm in their debt. These are all thoughts to be suppressed.

The Bible teaches that, yes, God is distant, but we have not been left alone. It says that God is distant, but that distance is of our own making. But there is still more to be said.

12

Is God Distant?

Part 3

It takes us quite a while to realize that things haven't always been the way we know them now. It takes time for our personal world to expand until it can take in other cultures and continents,[1] and in the same way we are slow to appreciate history.

I still remember the shock I felt the first day I needed to stay home from Mrs. King's kindergarten class. I had never consciously thought about it, but I suppose I had always assumed that while I was away at school everyone at home relaxed and smoked cigarettes like movie extras waiting to be called for their next scene. After all, I was the hero of the story and everyone else merely played a part in the drama of my life. I was taken aback that day I stayed home to find that a whole world went on that its existence I had never guessed. The phone rang, and so did

---

1. If ever we discover extraterrestrial life, it may again take us some time to adjust our picture of ourselves and our place as humans in reality.

the doorbell; down the road, Post Oak Pharmacy did a booming business, and in town people met for lunch. And, just as shockingly, when I finally was healthy and went back to school, I found that they had gone on in their lessons without me.

In a similar way, perhaps, we may assume that the processes we see at work in the world today have always been grinding away. It takes us quite a while to realize that the world hasn't always been the way we know it now. Yet evolutionary biologists assure us that today we are still driven by the same urges that drove our primitive ancestors—the urge to survive, the urge to propagate our genes as widely as possible.

We are less familiar with the tale the Bible tells about our changing world. It maintains that God is distant, as we experience today, but that He was not always so. Once, things were very different. In the beginning of the story, we find Him walking in the cool of the evening in the garden where He had put our first ancestors.

Some scholars might insist that Moses could not have written this passage in the book of Genesis—he could not have accepted the idea of God walking amongst people even as an oral tradition, let alone have invented it himself. In the book of Exodus we are told how Moses had to be hidden in a cleft of a rock, protected by God's hand, when the Divine passed by, because no one could see God's face and live. God is an utterly holy Being and exposure to Him is lethal to human beings. You just can't have God walking around in a garden in the cool of the evening.

But this idea of being near God would have troubled Moses only if he had ignored his own testimony that things have not always been as we know them now. Something drastic had changed between the story in Genesis and the one in Exodus. Today, like Moses, we have to be protected from God's presence just as we have to be shielded from a nuclear reactor; but there was a time when this was not so. Circumstances have not always been as we experience them; changes have occurred more radical than just incremental and quantitative developments obeying stable processes. Moses understood that God is holy, he understood that human beings have become unclean—in other words, he understood the idea of the sacred. But Moses also knew that if people had ever been holy they could have stood unprotected, unshielded, naked, and unashamed in the presence of God.

We want God to be near to us and the Bible proclaims that one day He will be, but this will happen only after the problem of the sacred is solved and people have become holy once again. The alternative would be for God to become unclean—but this would involve Him violating His nature and character, and I cannot imagine what might occur in that event. I suppose that even Heaven would become Hell if God chose that option. If He became unclean, the New Story would be true and we would have no hope for a better future.

It seems there is an awful symmetry about history: if there was no drastic shift in the distant past, then there is no great hope for a shift in the future. We can believe that we will be near God one day because it was possible once. It's right for us to be dissatisfied with our present world: we are coping with the in-between time. We hope for a city we have not yet seen, and we mourn the loss of a garden from which we were banished.

As an aside, many people throughout history have been unable to accept Jesus as the Christ because they misunderstood the problem of the sacred. They suspected that a *kenosis* and an incarnation must oblige God to become unclean in the process. You can't remain clean if you walk a muddy road. I am told that parts of Islam teach that Jesus only appeared to die on the cross. They find the idea that God could abandon a righteous prophet to an ignominious death disgraceful. They realize that in a sense God must be shielded from us as well. Even before Islam began, the second-century Christian author Theophilus wrote to explain how God could walk in Paradise when God was also said not to be contained in a place.[2]

I suppose that God could appear unveiled among us now, but because our common-sense theology doesn't sense the problem of the sacred, we do not grasp that this would have catastrophic effects. God will be fully revealed, but not until it is time to settle final accounts at the judgment. For Him to dwell among us now would be like an HIV-positive lover to have intercourse with his or her loved one without ensuring the protection of that loved one. This shocking simile works backwards, however, because here the infection is a consuming purity that destroys anything that is morally diseased. It is as if we could be killed by contact with someone healthy because we are so sick.

When the elf Arwen loved Aragorn in Tolkien's Middle Earth, she gave up her deathless state and became mortal to gain the man she loved. It's a highly romantic idea, but it's not what we want God to do in order to draw near to us. Instead, we want Him to take us up into the immortal, and this is His plan. The Christ was not made unclean by taking on our type of body. He wasn't sent to judge us but to live among us and to perfectly reveal the character of God. He became our servant, and then

2.   In *Theophilus to Autolychus* book II, chapter 22.

our victim. And God, the greatest of all storytellers, turned this worst of crimes into the means to end our alienation, the basis of our hoped-for reconciliation, our protection from His consuming goodness. Even as we protest that God has abandoned us and that we long for Him to draw near, we need to consider seriously the story of Jesus and what it says about us. We did not love the goodness when it came close to us. We suppressed it very crudely.

Those who sensed the problem of the sacred were troubled by the anointed visitor. Early in their acquaintance, Peter took Jesus out in his boat so that more of the crowd on the shore could see and hear the young rabbi. After listening to Jesus' words, we might have expected Peter to be full of relief and hope and joy, but we think this because we have such a poor grasp of the problem of the sacred. Instead, Peter was dismayed at the authority displayed in Jesus' miracles and, though he recognized the truth and goodness of Jesus' words, he asked the Christ to depart from him. Peter knew that he was unclean and unworthy to associate with someone holy. Jesus, however, was kind enough to refuse his request. Although his belief in Jesus and his teachings would later be the cause of Peter's execution, they were also the cause of his ultimate salvation.

In the film *Blade Runner,* a quartet of super bio-robots have turned renegade and have returned to Earth to find their maker and kill him. As the movie progresses, you begin to sympathize with these manufactured life-forms because their creator gave them desires they cannot fulfill. An expiration date has been programmed into them in order to keep them under human control and they are angry at the inevitability of their unnecessary death. This anger is the perspective of the New Story: God has been unkind. The Bible tells a very different story, however, and we must decide which is the truth. In *Blade Runner,* the problem of the sacred is that the creatures are good in themselves and their creator is afraid of them. In the Bible, the problem is that the creatures have gone bad—not so bad as to lose all value but bad enough to give them reason to be afraid to meet the Creator, even if they don't know this. God's distance is a kind of protection from things we can barely imagine.

God is distant, but we are not left alone in ignorance of His existence or His will. God is distant, because we have drawn away from Him by suppressing the truth and refusing to be thankful. But God is also distant because He is holy and we are not. At least, not yet. He has visited us as one of us, and we again proved ourselves unworthy of His friendship.

> He was in the world, and though the world was made through Him, the world did not recognize Him. He came to that which was His own, but His own did not receive Him.[3]

---

3. John 1:10–11.

13

Is God Distant?

Part 4

There are three things about Christianity I find very hard to believe. I don't have a huge problem with miracles such as a virgin birth or a resurrection, even though I know something of reproductive physiology and the process of necrosis. Once we allow that God exists, these things become credible. No, the stumbling blocks for me involve myself more intimately. I find it almost inconceivable that goodness is going to outlast evil. I have difficulty accepting that I can really change from the kind of person I am into someone holy. And hardest of all—because it seems absurd on the face of it, and presumptuous to the point of madness—is the idea that the God who exists dwells with me.

The distance between us and God that we experience is not the ordinary kind that is measured in space or even time. The Bible teaches that there is nowhere we can go to escape God's presence. Rather—though every metaphor has its limitations—the distance is more like that which occurs during a bad time in

a marriage. The man and woman share the same conditions—
they occupy the same living space, and even the same bed—but
we can understand that they are separate. In fact, their physical
proximity actually makes the distance between them all the more
tragic because although it may feel unbridgeable, it is not.

We also experience a distance because we have a problem
seeing. I remember cycling through the streets of Kathmandu
when I first went to live there. The small shops were covered in
signs, but because they were all in the Deva Nagri script they
were as good as invisible to me. After a few days of language
school, having learned the alphabet and its pronunciation, my
ride through the streets was a very different experience. Even
without all the necessary vocabulary, I found that the signs were
coming into focus. I even discovered that some of them were
actually in English.

Or again our distance from God is like our unawareness of
those parts of the electro-magnetic spectrum that flood the air
around us with images and messages we cannot access except
with the necessary technology.

It is like being on one side of a wall erected by a fundamental
change in our perceptions. Once, the world was full of gods and
marvels until the new stories told by Kepler, Copernicus, and
Galileo began to disenchant it. It is possible to re-enchant it with
God's presence without having to say that modern astronomy
is a lie—but it seems a difficult project. Perhaps we need walls,
but we have built them in the wrong places. Perhaps these have
ruined the habitat and caused an unnecessary disenchantment.

The distance I feel between me and God is like those occa-
sions when I know I should apologize to my daughter after los-
ing my temper and speaking to her sarcastically. The six inches

between my hand and hers on the breakfast table might as well be miles of hostile trenches and barbed wire.

How far is it between my desire for life and my fears and my pride? How far from the truth is a lie? How far is trust from suspicion? How far from Jesus was Pilate sitting when he asked, "What is truth?"

Overcoming the distance is different for different people, but there is only one way it can be done. We encounter this sort of thing elsewhere: a mother may love her son, and love is one—and yet love can be expressed in as many ways as there are sons and mothers. This is just one way of saying that there is no normative spiritual experience but there is normative theology. It would do us no good for God to pretend that He was just any way, instead of the particular person He is. Allowing us to keep our idols, though it may seem an easy option, is just not in His character—which is the same as saying that it would not be loving.

I had gone to church for most of my life, in the kind of church that quoted from the Bible constantly and spoke every Sunday of the need to be reconciled with God—and yet it felt as if I had never heard the message before on the day that the distance closed and God came to dwell with me.

If you get married, you are married—and yet it's also just a beginning. God's Spirit does live in me. I am united with the Christ in his death and resurrection, though at times it seems the most outrageous claim to make, even to myself—perhaps especially to myself.

I have begun the pilgrimage to the Holy Kingdom, but sometimes I grow discouraged. What looked like the final ridge turns out to have been hiding many more behind it. Sometimes

I would rather sit down and feel sorry for myself. Deeper visions of my heart and my motives that come with time are not encouraging. Sometimes I'm not so sure that I want to leave behind the familiar landscape of weeds and anthills, even for the promise of a land of wine and olives.

God is near, and we can experience His nearness in this life, but never perfectly: the various distances creep back in. I see Him as I see my wife, or my daughter, or the stars, or the signs along the streets of Kathmandu.

14

Is God a Bully?

Part 1

Why should we listen to God when He tells us what we should do? Is our only motivation to obey our fear of being punished? Is the sole source of God's authority over us His power?

All our books and movies tell us that power is not enough to warrant authority. Our legends usually follow the formula that power resides with the bad guys and the good guys are weak. It is therefore right to struggle against authority. Tyrants need to be overthrown. It is something of a ruling metaphor in the culture I grew up in. Robin Hood is an outlaw against John (until King Richard returns from abroad). Zorro swashbuckles through California until the greedy dons surrender their power to the people. We think it pathological when a hostage begins to love her tormentors.

Have we been taken hostage by God? Is morality the demands of the hijacker, "Do exactly what I say and nobody will get hurt'? And after delivering this ultimatum to the whole world, does God have the nerve to expect us to love Him?

In a conversation around a lunch table, a group of us discussed what we wanted from a church. For those of us who were not actually interested in church, the question changed to what could make them want to participate in the life of such an institution. One earnest young man said that he looked for a community that "helped him to mature in his relationship with God."

Talk of "maturity" can be a cliché among Christians, but maybe it doesn't have to be. If we examine the notion of maturing, I think it can help to answer our suspicions that God's rule is no better than that of the bully in the back seat of the school bus. The question I would put to the earnest young man would be, Do immature people know what they are seeking when they say they wish to mature? One aspect of immaturity seems to be that we don't know what we should do in order to become all we are meant to be. Another seems to be that we lack the wisdom to do what we know we need to in order to mature.

Though the immature may have an idea of where they mean to go in life, they will realize one day when they are further down the road that they had a very poor grasp of the goal they were heading toward. I remember quite vividly (and with some embarrassment) an occasion when I was twelve. I was walking down the hallway of my elementary school. It was my last year there: everyone knew my name, I had won every award for popularity, and my grades were high. I remember that I was alone, so I may have been returning to my class from a meeting with the principal as the student fire chief. And as I walked, with the sun shining in my eyes, I was thinking with satisfaction about my maturity. I realized that at twelve I still had some growing to do—I ought to get a bit taller—but I thought that, all things considered, I really knew just about everything I needed to. Further maturing was mostly a matter of gaining height.

I appreciate now, of course, that that twelve-year-old had a very slight acquaintance not just with experience but with a great deal of things of worth and purpose. For example, he had learned how to succeed in pleasing a certain kind of person, but he knew very little about the important matter of *not* pleasing people. I was satisfied before I should have been. Had I been able to do so, I would have stopped the process of maturing.

This process of maturing seems to be about learning to do things that are not natural. Someone more mature than us helps us to do the things necessary to attain our goals, or to replace them with even better goals previously unsuspected by us. This may involve a degree of compulsion, especially at first when we do not see that what feels like an unnatural effort is required to build the muscle we long for. Here is the point at which to bring in all the worries and complaints older people have about the mindset of "instant gratification" they claim to see in younger people, who, they worry, will not show the wisdom to make the efforts necessary to mature.

The process of maturing can feel natural and it can feel very unnatural, but you wouldn't want to compel a thirty-year-old to eat his broccoli the way you might be willing to make a seven-year-old. Adolescence is a painful time for everyone involved (though often teenagers are not mature enough to take seriously their parents' suffering, or anyone else's except their own). Hopefully, the parents are themselves maturing. Yet even the

best ones—or perhaps, especially the best ones—have difficulty
in letting their children become independent.

Dorothee Soelle is a theologian who advocates changing Christianity because of the suspicions of the New Story.
She thinks that an authoritarian religion keeps people from
maturing.

> Authoritarian religion . . . is characterized by three
> structural elements:
>
> - Recognition of a higher power that holds
>   our fate in its hands and excludes any
>   self-determination.
>
> - Submission to the rule of this power, which
>   needs no moral legitimation such as love or
>   justice.
>
> - A deep pessimism about the human person:
>   he or she is not capable of love or truth, but is
>   a powerless and meaningless being whose obe-
>   dience feeds on the very denial of his or her
>   own strength.
>
> The main virtue in authoritarian religion is obedience;
> its cardinal sin is rebellion, in contrast to humanitarian
> religion, which moves self-actualization and lapses of
> the self to center stage.[1]

Follow this criticism carefully. Soelle's words are a potent
accusation against a god who bases his authority on power and
knowledge, which is what she means by "authoritarian religion."

---

1. D. Soelle, *Theology for Skeptics*, Fortress Press, 1995, p21.

She thinks that a powerful god and authoritarian religion are bad for people and keep us from realizing our potential. Such a god stunts our growth and leaves us like the thirty-year-old still forced to eat his broccoli.

The New Story suspects that this description matches the God of the Bible. An omnipotent God is like unblinking Fate: we are powerless before Him, determined from outside ourselves. It doesn't matter what we do—and no one can mature if their actions do not matter. This is what the movies mean when they represent rich people as spoiled and immature—their money makes it seem that their actions don't matter. They can buy their way out of undesirable consequences to themselves. They don't have to grow up.

An all-powerful God has His way with us and doesn't have to earn the right to be obeyed. And when might makes right, no one is going to mature: we all remain slaves. If we keep our heads down and do what we're told, maybe we'll escape notice and we won't be sent to Siberia.

A holy God keeps us immature by insisting that we only do those things He approves of. There is no goodness in us—all goodness resides in God. This is the pessimism that Soelle thinks prevents human growth towards love and responsibility. She contrasts this with a humanitarian religion that moves away from categories of sin and rebellion and towards maturity of the self. Such a religion is a large part of our contemporary common-sense theology.

Perhaps these ideas are true of "authoritarian religion." There are families in which the children are so controlled by their parents that the very things the parents hope to cultivate in them never develop. But is biblical religion authoritarian in this way?

I don't think so, and I believe it's a very serious mistake, with gigantic ramifications, to suppose that these particular criticisms apply to the God of the Bible.

Let me begin with Soelle's last observation: that the main virtue in authoritarian religion is obedience and its cardinal sin is rebellion. As a veterinarian in Nepal I would sometimes be called on to treat cows. Nepal was, at the time, the world's only officially Hindu state, and as a Jesuit scholar once said to me, "trying to study Hinduism is like trying to shovel mist." It has no creed or council or pope, and its scriptures are accepted by some but not others. However, most books on comparative religion identify five or six characteristic practices, and one of these is the veneration of cows. Nepalese law took willful harm to a cow as seriously as similar harm to a human being. It meant that treating a sick cow was a risky affair, because if the beast died under my care I could conceivably be charged with murder. I would give a water buffalo an injection of antibiotic without a qualm, but if I did the same to a cow, I might hear villagers muttering as I plunged an eighteen-gauge needle into her flank.

To violate a cow in any way, regardless of the motivation, could be interpreted as a sin. This is an example of religion where obedience is all that matters. The notion of sin in rural Nepal was to break a rule of ritual. This is surprising to us, because we don't usually think of Hinduism as particularly authoritarian.

In my early years as a Christian, I thought of sin in very similar terms. There was a god with a moral will and I had violated that will. My problem was disobedience, or, to use Soelle's terminology, rebellion. The essence of sin was defiance of God's will, and therefore the answer was obedience. I was rebelling and

I needed to stop. The root cause of my alienation from God was that I didn't do what He commanded.

I grew uncomfortable with this theology, however, because I found in time that my understanding seemed to be at odds with what the Bible taught, "the just shall live by faith." In what possible way could trust be the answer to my problem of disobedience? I began to suspect that biblical religion had an unsolvable contradiction at its very center. But when I carefully observed what I had always called my "sin" I found that, prior to defying what I understood of God's will, I had already disbelieved Him.

It was difficult to see this at first because everything happens so quickly. It was like watching the diving events at the Olympics on television. In real time, the divers seemed to perform miracles of disciplined precision; but afterwards the commentators, usually former divers themselves, would immediately criticize their performance. I used to be irritated by this. It had looked perfect to me—could they do any better? Yet when they showed the slow-motion replay, I saw that the commentators were correct: not everything had been executed perfectly. The feet weren't together when she hit the water, her right arm wasn't quite back in position, the twist was only partly complete.

In much the same way, when I slowed down the process of disobeying God I could see something I hadn't noticed before because of the speed and the splash. I saw the element of distrust that always preceded my disobedience. I found that before I sinned, by omission or commission, I had chosen not to trust God, and I saw that I'd chosen not to trust Him in two ways. First, I doubted that He understood my situation. If God were me, I reasoned with the blinding speed born of habit, He would see my desires my way and relent. I didn't trust God as my Creator and I thought that I was the expert on my fulfillment and self-actualization. God asked me to do something contrary to my desires because He didn't understand me.

Second, I distrusted His intentions for me. I thought He forbade certain things or commanded others because He didn't have my happiness and flourishing in mind. In other words, I doubted His love, concern and goodness. The things I desired promised me happiness and a way to avoid pain. If God was against these things it must be because He couldn't be trusted to want me to be happy and free from pain. Each time I disobeyed, I considered myself more of an expert than God on what pleases me, and I certainly thought I could trust myself more than Him to look after my happiness.

If these observations are true, my problem of distrust is more fundamental than my problem of disobedience. The essence of sin is not disobedience but distrust. My alienation from God is due to my distrust. If I want to change, I need to begin by learning to trust God, because he is my Creator and because his intentions towards me are kind, rather than concentrating exclusively on my behavior. This is what I find the Bible says when read carefully. The temptations it describes first attack our trust of God's understanding and goodness.

> "You will not surely die," the serpent said to the woman. "For God knows that when you eat of it your eyes will be opened, and you will be like God, knowing good and evil."

> When the woman saw that the fruit of the tree was good for food and pleasing to the eye, and also desirable for gaining wisdom, she took

some and ate it. She also gave some to her husband, who was with her, and he ate it.[2]

I would say that as I have matured I have found the Bible
to be ever more consistent and more psychologically exquisite.
The main virtue of biblical religion is trust in God and its cardinal sin is distrust. I couldn't see this dynamic when I was less
mature.

---

2. Genesis 3:4–6.

15

Is God a Bully?

Part 2

God knows what we should do morally: in bed and in business, in our words and our actions, in our ambitions and our longings. He can't help Himself. If I may use shocking language, it's a problem He has.

We might be grateful for this characteristic of God, but much of our common-sense theology is exasperated by it. We think it both belittles Him and limits us. We want a god as mature and open as we are: one who appreciates that morality is infinitely relative and so we must tolerate conflicting notions of what is right, in different people and different cultures. If we're going to mature as people, we cannot just accept what God once told us to do as if He still tells us to do it. Things must evolve and progress. Without the freedom to change, it's impossible to grow. How are we to grow into mature people if God has the authority to tell us what to do and we just accept it?

Perhaps we would expect people to be glad if God were to tell us His will. After all, they might find it helpful—it could alleviate their pain and give them some sense of purpose. But that is not our reaction to revelation nowadays. A little over a year after the attack on the World Trade Center, the historian Simon Schama wrote in the *Guardian* about American's understanding before that devastating day:

> [It] was already commendably clear on what the battle lines of the already bloody new century would be: the conflict between those who not only claimed a monopoly of wisdom, but the right to impose it on everyone else, against those who claimed neither. Put another way, the fight is between power based on revelation (and thus not open to argument) and power based on persuasion (and thus conditional on argument): militant theocracy against the tolerant Enlightenment. . . . For the most part, though, to say out loud (as a few courageous souls have done) that religious revelation— Judaic and Christian as well as Muslim, not least the notion of paradise for the pure—is the problem is to risk immediate and irrevocable patriotic anathema.[1]

We are suspicious of authority that is based upon power alone rather than on love and justice. We are also suspicious of power that is based on revelation, whatever the source, because

---

1. *The Guardian Weekly*, 19 September 2002.

we believe that all revelations make the same claim to authority and can't be distinguished from each other. And Paradise—that better future in which previous generations once placed their hope—we now see as our problem rather than our answer.

In a classroom discussion on the authority of the Bible, I was surprised by the intensity of the antagonism to "authority" expressed by the students. The occasion was another of my unscientific word associations. Those who responded said it made them think of inequality and loss of control, though several allowed that authority was acceptable if it was "in a relationship but not institutionalized." One student characterized authority as "stupid people over smart people."

No authority based on power alone, no power backed up by the authority of revelation—these principles are fundamental to our contemporary common-sense theology. And they render us helpless in knowing and hearing and obeying the God who exists and can speak and wishes us well. We have a deep problem with authority—and yet we cannot live without giving authority to something or someone, even if it's to the tolerant Enlightenment and its method of persuasive argument.

It reminds me, strangely enough, of the movie *School of Rock.* Jack Black plays a guitarist who has been kicked out of his band and, in need of some money, gets a job teaching at a posh private school. He knows very little about anything except the history and ethos of rock 'n' roll, and is stunned to find that his pupils know nothing about the only thing in the world that seems worthwhile to him. Predictably, he starts to turn them into a band, without the knowledge or approval of the school's administration or their parents. My children loved the film. Watching it with them, I felt like the Tsar standing incognito among a crowd of factory-workers listening to a speech by Lenin.

What I find poignant is that the guitarist tells his class that the very heart of rock is to disrespect "the Man"—that is, the establishment, or anyone who holds power. Two-thirds of the way through the movie, he realizes that for them he himself is the Man, and so he invites them to diss him. However, in one very clever and comic exchange, he has to tell a pupil who takes him up on the offer that there are limits to the disrespect allowed and he demands that his authority be recognized when he wants it to be. The class acquiesces—they realize that someone has to have authority. But what if they hadn't? *School of Rock* might have mutated into *The Lord of the Flies*, and it would no longer have been funny.

I don't come from a respectful Asian culture, but from the West. My culture teaches me that I have a duty to stand up to bullies and tyrants. We remember the lesson from the Nuremberg trials of Nazi war criminals, that it is the responsibility of a subordinate to judge the dictates of an authority, any authority—and we have added "even a divine authority." We no longer see any nobility in the patriarch, Abraham, trekking off at God's command, with firewood and a knife, to offer up his son Isaac on an altar, unaware that God intended to stay his hand at the last moment.

My culture gives me a love for the underdog: the team of misfit hockey-players that makes it to the Olympics and beats the Russians and their state-sponsored efficiency or the poor Lithuanians who beat the multi-million-dollar American "dream team" at basketball. Bill Gates of Microsoft was popular so long as he was the epitome of the little guy overcoming the odds to achieve success; but as soon as we begin to see him as a giant, we feel a duty to despise him and chop down the beanstalk.

In my culture, we are happiest when we can tell ourselves that the locus of tyrannical power is one lone bad guy. It makes things so much simpler: just defeat that one evil and everything resolves into peaceful coexistence.

So, if I suspect that God is a tyrant, I will consider it my duty to stand up for my rights against Him. I'll be heroic in my rebellion, like Prometheus defying the will of Zeus to help humankind. After all, God is never an underdog—He's almighty. Surely He's the ultimate tyrant? This suspicion, strengthened by my culture's assumptions, injects a cold vapor into the center of my heart where my love for God tries to thrive.

Of course might is a source of some kind of authority, and it produces fear. This is what Thomas Hobbes, of the tolerant Enlightenment, called "the state of nature." This is what Mao Zedong meant when he famously said that "power comes out of the barrel of a gun."

We also give authority away, not because we are afraid but because we recognize the abilities of someone or something else. In the original *Star Wars*, Luke Skywalker turns off his targeting computer when he decides to "listen to the Force." He makes this counter-intuitive decision not irrationally but because he believes that the Force is better able than his computer to put his bomb down the little ventilator shaft of the Death Star. We have an uncomfortable relationship with expertise today, but we rely on it heavily as a source of authority.

We often assign authority and think that this is the best solution. If we assign it, it helps us to believe that we are its source. This is one reason the West feels that it occupies the high moral

ground when it promotes democracy to the rest of the world. We
elect our authorities by finding the will of the people through
the ballot box. We think that the market identifies or expresses
people's priorities through free consumer choice, and on that
basis we instruct our officials to watch over it to ensure that no
monopoly constrains its freedom or undermines its power to
decide.

However, we can also give authority on the basis of roles
and relationships and traditions. In the last episode of the TV
series *Band of Brothers*, Major Dick Winters is sitting in a Jeep
when he sees his former instructor passing by. This man had
tyrannized Winters in basic training, but that was before D-Day
and the long months of combat and bloodshed that followed
it, and Winters is now the more experienced soldier as well as
the senior officer. The instructor makes as if to walk by without
acknowledging him, but Winters calls out to him to demand the
protocol of respect, "We salute the rank, not the man." In other
words, the instructor owed this respect, and it was not a point of
pride or revenge.

Whenever I asked my neighbors in Nepal to explain a particular festival to me, the usual answer was, "This is how our
people have always done this." In *Fiddler on the Roof*, a musi-
cal that wrestles with the place and the limits of tradition, the
Jewish milkman Tevye keeps insisting to his daughters, "I am
your father! I'm the papa!" and expects this fact to carry great
weight. It doesn't, but he thinks that it should.

The West is unsure of the place of roles and relationships
and traditions in how we assign authority. I find it very intriguing that evangelical Christians, some of whom once ascribed religious authority to "the Bible alone," now seem to have found

this unsatisfactory and are exploring older forms of Christianity that predate the tolerant Enlightenment.

We grant authority to power and ability (and nowadays also to celebrity), we attach it to the decisions of voters and consumers and we give it to tradition; but we also believe that authority can be earned by character and wisdom. Why, for example, did the late twentieth century give such authority to Nelson Mandela? It wasn't just because he became famous as the first elected black president of South Africa, but that he spent a lifetime in selfless sacrifice to achieve the abolition of apartheid and reconciliation in South Africa. We listen to him with respect: he has earned it.

Can we use the example of human authority to gain any insight into the problem of God's power? It is only a limited help, because it's only an analogy, but I think that it can aid us to circumvent some of our prejudices.

The God who exists is not a bully, though He has difficulty showing this through the veils of our common-sense theology. He doesn't use His power merely to assert Himself, but he is the source of power (given that He is the Creator and the ground of all being and morality). It's best that it is in relation to God that we find our place in the universe, for He is the one point that is not merely relative to every other point.

Nor does God use His authority for personal gain. But given that He is the Creator and the ground of all being and morality, it is best when His will is done. Everything that is truly good and beautiful will prove to please Him, and this is the nearest we can get to saying that it is for God's "benefit."

It's true that God is powerful. This is an inescapable fact and the Bible doesn't try to avoid the subject—in fact, it teaches that it is wise to fear the Almighty. Yet we are also urged by the

Scriptures to meet Him in His mercy as adopted children rather
than in His impartial anger against all evil.

We do not assign God His authority in the sense that it
wouldn't belong to Him unless we gave it to Him; and yet here
our language fails us slightly. We can *recognize* His authority,
and this makes an enormous difference in our relationship both
to Him and to other people, for God isn't interested only in the
happiness of individuals but also in the flourishing of families
and peoples and cultures.

God's abilities exceed anyone else's and yet, to please Him and
to help us to mature, He entrusts many things to us. Obviously,
we don't always do very well at the tasks we've been given, and
in Psalm 8 the author marvels at God's audacity in entrusting so
much to a race so immature:

> What is man that you are mindful of him,
>   the son of man that you care for him?
>
> You made him a little lower than the heavenly
> beings
>   and crowned him with glory and honor.
>
> You made him ruler over the works of your
> hands;
>   you put everything under his feet:
>
> all flocks and herds,
>   and the beasts of the field,
>
> the birds of the air,
>   and the fish of the sea,
>   all that swim the paths of the seas.[2]

---

2. Psalm 8:4–8. "Man" here, of course, embraces both genders.

We have been given so much responsibility over our world. It's like the first time a parent slides over to the passenger seat to let their teenager sit behind the wheel and put the car into gear. We give back to God authority which came from Him in the first place, and He gives us authority that He could wield much better than we do and yet He does it for our good and for His pleasure.

However, we haven't elected God as our authority. Just because Christianity has more adherents than any other religion doesn't make it true or prove that its God exists. To think that we vote with our faith and thereby establish truth is to play with reality in a very immature way and to "speak from below," as if we determined reality rather than having to learn what it is and then learn how to deal with it successfully.

The analogy of the sources of human authority may help us to see that God cannot always behave in the way we would like Him to. He has power that no one has given to Him, and then, to help us to mature, gives us responsibilities we are not quite up to. We would be wise to ask Him for guidance on how we should live with one another, and yet (as children so often do) we really hate it when He tells us what is right. We shake our little fists and say He doesn't trust us. We think we have a right to our sexuality, our business ethics, our mitigating circumstances. We don't think there should be any guilt apportioned except that which we recognize ourselves.

The analogy might help, but it doesn't really capture our imaginations. We might give it our grudging mental assent, but it doesn't command our hearts. And that leaves us as grumpy subjects, like the citizens of a great democracy who don't bother to vote but avail themselves of their right to complain. It is in the story of the *kenosis* and the incarnation that we see that God manages (despite being the source of all power and authority) to *earn* His power and authority. It is a move of genius.

Emmanuel is the best revelation of the nature and character of the God who exists, even though the Christ took the form of a servant. Dorothee Soelle wants to create a humanitarian religion, getting rid of the God of power and replacing Him with

> a God who is sad like us, small like us, without
> bank accounts and bombs.[3]

This sounds inviting, but do we really want a god as sad and small as we are? I think what we long for is a God who can empathize with our smallness and yet doesn't have our myriad weaknesses. We desire compassion and comfort, but we also need to be rescued. It does no good if the lifeboat itself is sinking. Jesus, however, on the night before his execution, a night on which we could forgive anyone for being a bit self-absorbed, celebrates—even fulfills—the Passover feast. He washes the feet of His disciples, even the one who is going to betray him to his enemies with a kiss.

> "Do you understand what I have done for
> you?" he asked them. "You call me 'Teacher'
> and 'Lord,' and rightly so, for that is what I
> am. Now that I, your Lord and Teacher, have
> washed your feet, you also should wash one
> another's feet. I have set you an example that
> you should do as I have done for you."[4]

---

3. Dorothee Soelle, *Theology for Skeptics*, Fortress Press, 1995, p44.
4. John 13:12–15.

In the form of a servant, the Christ managed to earn his authority and the right to use his power:

> Whoever wants to become great among you must be your servant, and whoever wants to be first must be slave of all. For even the Son of Man did not come to be served, but to serve, and to give his life as a ransom for many.[5]

It is this same servant of whom the ancient creeds say, "He rose again on the third day and was seated at the right hand of God the Father, from thence he shall come to judge the living and the dead." It was after his resurrection that Jesus tells his followers:

> All authority in heaven and on earth has been given to me.[6]

God has solved the problem by earning in history the power and authority to teach us how to live. He has managed to do it in such a way that we can mature best by listening to Him. Even at His weakest, God is shown to be powerful.

---

5. Mark 10:43–45.

6. Matthew 28:18.

16

Is God a Bully?

Part 3

My children like to ask questions. They do so usually to get answers, and this is good and healthy behavior that will help them to grow in knowledge about the world and how it works. But they can ask questions with another agenda entirely.

"Gillian, it's time for bed now."

"Why?"

(This could be a genuine question. We can tell if it is by how she reacts to the answer.)

"Well, it's 10 o'clock, and it's a school night, so it's bedtime."

"Why?"

(It's hard to put this down in print, because so much of the deep purpose of a question is communicated by the way it's said. One of the great and rarely acknowledged difficulties of being a follower of Jesus is not knowing in what tone of voice he said some of the things recorded in the Bible.)

"Well, we've learned that you need about nine hours of sleep to feel good the next day. Otherwise, you're tired and grumpy and the morning is unpleasant for everybody."

"Oh, so this is about making you happy, then?"

(Here a certain distrust is evident, or maybe the questioner is just trying to pretend to be moral in order to get her own way. I may respond badly to her suspicion, and I may be embarrassed if her suspicion is partly justified.)

"No, this isn't about just pleasing me. You don't seem happy when you don't get enough sleep, and you're unkind to the rest of the family. So, it's time for bed!"

"Why?"

(My own tone of voice at this point often becomes less loving than it should be.)

"All right, young lady, if you don't go upstairs right now and put on your pajamas, then Jenny will not be allowed to come over after school tomorrow."

"Why? What have I done? I was just asking questions!"

What was meant to be loving has degenerated into the threat of punishment, or even force, in response to a test of power. I am not in any way pretending to be a very skillful parent; sometimes I misinterpret the deep meaning of a question, sometimes I try to control something best left to a maturing child. Sometimes my pretense of love really is about making me happy. Nevertheless, one thing is clear to me: we can ask questions long after they have ceased to do us any good. Perhaps we can also attempt to answer them long after it has ceased to serve any useful purpose.

Increasingly, it seems to me that we need no longer feel obliged to answer questions once we have shown that our action or our request is based on love. Once I show Gillian that my instruction to go to bed is based in love, she can continue to ask questions and to distrust me, for sure, but the power of her questions to compel me to answer is diminished.

The Devil is in the details, of course. The tricky bit is the "once I show Gillian." I may think my request is reasonable and is obviously prompted by my love for her and the rest of the family, but she honestly may not yet see it as such. In that case, she may continue to interrogate me, and I would be wise to take her questions seriously.

On the other hand, they may express a denial of my love, a rejection of my authority, a suspicion of my motives—even a will to suspicion. Being a parent, a tired parent and a tired parent whose relationship with his daughter is habit-bound, I may not be a perfect judge of when my daughter's questions are innocent and when their deep purpose is something other than to seek reassurance that I love her.

Gillian, too, may be tired and her relationship with me also has its habits. She may once have accepted that the answers to her questions were informed by love, but as she has grown older, new thoughts may have occurred to her and new doubts arisen. We may have to revisit earlier conversations and retrace the thread to love. Sometimes as she matures she begins to see that she was right to trust me before. Sadly, there may be other times when she sees that she shouldn't have trusted me, because I wasn't motivated by love.

Thankfully, when we deal with God we are dealing with someone who knows where the boundary lies between honest confusion and willful, self-serving suspicion. It's true that the conversation is odd and usually feels very one-sided. When we question the intentions behind God's moral will for us, He knows whether we are in earnest or we don't want to know and find it convenient not to understand. He even knows this better than we do, because we are so good at concealing the truth from ourselves.

Jesus was fairly clear on this, and on one occasion I believe we can sense the tone of his words:

> Which of you fathers, if your son asks for a fish, will give him a snake instead? Or if he asks for an egg, will give him a scorpion? If you then, though you are evil, know how to give good gifts to your children, how much more will your Father in heaven give the Holy Spirit to those who ask him![1]

These words, however, may not be welcome to us. We have been disappointed in the past, our expectations have not been fulfilled, and at times we have been given snakes and scorpions. If we are honest, we may not even want to be given the Holy Spirit.

The promise in Jesus' words—and it is no good protecting God from our disappointment by pretending that this isn't a promise—is that we can have God's presence with us, hearts to love as the Christ taught us to, and eyes to see what is really treasure and what is not. We still have to cooperate with the Spirit, first by trusting and then by obeying; but the Spirit is not just human religious psychosis. It isn't just a case of feeling as if God is with us.

---

1. Luke 11:11–13.

In our common-sense theology, the Trinity is not a priority at present, but this is something we need to reconsider. We need God as Creator and Judge. We need God to empty Himself in *kenosis* and become incarnate. We need God as Spirit to dwell with us in the present and (as we learn to hope for it) the future.

God's moral will has a purpose. His goal for us—and as we mature, it becomes more and more our goal, too—is for us to become conformed to the image of the Christ, to experience union with the Christ. This is how we are reconciled with our Creator. This is how the problem of the sacred is solved. This is our imagined better future: increasingly changed to be all we are meant to be. The goodness we are to attain is not something vague or ambiguous, an image of something without a name. We are going to be holy in the same way that the Christ is holy—and yet we shall remain ourselves, because our problem is not that we are not God but that we aren't yet fully human, fully conformed to the image of God.

Some of us don't yet see that this is the only future that is really hopeful, and that it's a "better hope" because when the future arrives it will be true. We can talk about it and question it, and we can seek to persuade each other. It isn't foolish to rely on revelation to know things that only God can know with certainty. We are right to ask our questions, but there are many things we can ask that we cannot answer by starting from ourselves. Often we have to be told the answer. This is especially true when we are querying the desires and intentions of another being. We can guess what they are up to, but really we need them to tell us and to tell us in a way we can trust. This is part of why God reveals Himself through a book as well as through subjective religious experiences.

Ignatius was Bishop of Antioch in the second century, a period when it was not safe to be a bishop. As he was transported to Rome for execution for following the Christ, he wrote to those who loved him and mourned for him:

> Now I am beginning to be a disciple. May nothing seen or unseen grudge my attaining to Jesus Christ! Let fire and cross, encounters with wild animals, tearing apart of bones, hacking of limbs, crushing of the whole body, tortures of the Devil come upon me, if only I may attain to Jesus Christ!

This may sound morbid to us, but I think it is understandable. We all must die without exception. Ignatius believed that he saw the goal: to be conformed to the image of the Christ, to experience union with the Christ. His assurance didn't turn him into a fanatic willing to kill for the truth, as our common-sense theology fears that any such sense of certainty must. It did, however, make him willing to die at the hands of others.

Irenaeus, another second-century bishop, quoted Ignatius elsewhere as saying:

> I am God's wheat, ground by the teeth of beasts, that I may be found pure bread.

17

A Short Word on Exclusivity

Despite the religious and cultural diversity of his day, we rarely read of Jesus being involved in the kind of cross-cultural encounter I can have as I walk around London or I can see when I watch cable news. We can easily make the mistake of thinking that the Jewish God was the sort of harsh tribal deity that deserts generate and that Jesus was narrow-minded in the way people can be who have never traveled far from home.

One of the few such encounters the Bible relates does to some extent address our suspicion that God is exclusive in an unmerciful and immoral way. Exclusion from a job or a nightclub on the grounds of race, color, sexual preference, or creed is outlawed in liberal democracies; why should God exclude anyone from a relationship with Him on the basis of their beliefs?

Whether or not you are familiar with the story told in John 4, I would encourage you to read it, or read it again, very carefully.

Jesus was drawing crowds in the south of his country, but he decided to go back to the north, to the Galilee area where he grew up. Now, the journey required him to make a decision: either to travel through Samaria or to go the long way round it. Devout Jews at that time despised the Samaritans, and the more devout the Jew the more intense their dislike. (It was this prejudice that made the parable of the "good" Samaritan so infuriating to Jesus' Jewish audience.) And, as sometimes happens, this hatred had arisen not because the two peoples were profoundly different but because they had so much in common. The Samaritans were the nearest thing to the Jews in religion and culture in the pagan milieu of the first-century Mediterranean. Their ancestors were the Jews left behind when the elite of Judah were taken into captivity by the Babylonians in the sixth century BC, who had then intermarried with the surrounding peoples.

Jesus decides to take the direct route, through Samaria, and as he is walking one day with a group of his students he gets tired and rests at a celebrated well while his companions go off to buy food. It is probably necessary that he is alone for the encounter to occur—his disciples would have prevented it.

A Samaritan woman comes to the well to draw water, a perfectly normal and everyday thing to do. She doesn't say a word to the solitary man she finds there—in these parts women don't speak to strange men in any event, and she would know that Jewish rabbis think it defiles them to talk to Samaritans. She is also not the sort of woman religious people respect and, though the rabbi can't know that her sexual relationships are a long and messy tale, she knows it.

The Jew asks her for a drink of water, however. It is an intimate thing to do by the rules of that culture, not unlike me asking a woman I don't know at the pub if I can buy her a drink. The woman is very surprised. The rabbi has broken all sorts of solid cultural expectations. His behavior is shocking. His enemies could use it as proof of his unsuitability to be a teacher. The man is a bad example.

At first, the conversation is strained, as the two miss each other's meaning almost entirely. The woman pretends to a dull literalness and the rabbi talks in puzzling, mystical terms about "living water." But when the woman begins to be more responsive, Jesus asks her to call her husband before he goes on with the lesson.

The reader doesn't yet know what effect this request has on the woman—this emerges only slowly. In fact, it shames her. She doesn't want to admit this to the strange foreign rabbi and so she merely offers that she has no husband.

> Jesus said to her, "You are right when you say
> you have no husband. The fact is, you have had
> five husbands, and the man you now have is
> not your husband. What you have just said is
> quite true."

He is being ironic—after all, she wasn't very "right" in what she said—and yet he is kind. He asked the question not to trap her but to give her the opportunity to be honest. He accepts even her poor attempt to hide from him. Hers has been a very long and very sad story. Life in a small Samaritan village would have been difficult for her. The respectable men would have treated her with self-righteous disdain, but secretly they would have fantasized about her, knowing she was easy. The other women would have hated her, fearing her as a threat, but they may also have envied her liberty. This is why we find her drawing water at a time of day when the well is deserted: the other women like to congregate there in the morning and have a chat before they start their chores.

Jesus seems to know all this, and yet he doesn't seem purse-lipped and disapproving as she would expect a Galilean holy man to be.

> Sir, I can see that you are a prophet.

There's no point trying to hide anything from this strange man. How can he know so much about her? So, she changes the subject—and talks religion. She resorts to the usual, imponderable questions that always divide Jews and Samaritans, questions that never elicit answers but only hard-shelled prejudices. A rabbi should want to talk about that kind of stuff, and it also gets the conversation safely off the subject of her personal life. She continues:

> Our fathers worshiped on this mountain, but
> you Jews claim that the place where we must
> worship is in Jerusalem.

There, now they can have a comfortable argument along the usual well-worn cultural and religious footpaths. They can debate traditions and forms of religion. They can lose themselves in the disagreements of generations. She knows what even a Jewish prophet will have to say about these matters.

> Jesus declared, "Believe me, woman, a time is
> coming when you will worship the Father nei-

ther on this mountain nor in Jerusalem. Yet a
time is coming and has now come when the
true worshippers will worship the Father in
spirit and truth, for they are the kind of worshippers the Father seeks. God is spirit, and
his worshippers must worship in spirit and in
truth."

The rabbi takes the bait. This is a cross-cultural success
according to our common-sense theology. The old gives way
to the new. Forms and traditions give way to spiritual reality.
Acceptance overwhelms exclusivity. We can choose any path so
long as we are in earnest and have integrity.

I have written as if the story has the shape of a megaphone:
it begins narrowly, with religious intolerance and exclusion, and
it expands until it embraces everyone who is sincere. However,
I have been an unfaithful scribe. The story does end on a note
of inclusion, spiritual reality does prevail over empty observance
that can do nothing to reconcile us to the sacred—but I left
out a verse in the middle of the passage. The full text reads as
follows:

Jesus declared, "Believe me, woman, a time is
coming when you will worship the Father neither on this mountain nor in Jerusalem. You
Samaritans worship what you do not know;
we worship what we do know, for salvation is
from the Jews. Yet a time is coming and has
now come when the true worshippers will worship the Father in spirit and truth, for they are
the kind of worshippers the Father seeks. God

is spirit, and his worshippers must worship in
spirit and in truth."

The inclusiveness is there in the words, but not at the ex-
pense of constricting reality. We must be sincere, but we must
also be correct. Aspirin will not cure a little girl of tuberculosis,
however much I may want it to. We must have the right treatment for the disease as well as the good intention to cure it. And
our particular disease is alienation from the God who exists. We
are alienated by our distrust and our disobedience. Jesus knows
the right treatment for this disease and in saying so he is not being cruel; he is being kind.

He says that salvation is from the Jews, not from cultural
pride but because the Jews will indeed provide the means to
rescue us all from frustration and decay. He says that salvation is
from the Jews because he himself is a Jew.

The woman said, "I know that Messiah" (called
Christ) "is coming. When he comes, he will
explain everything to us."

Then Jesus declared, "I who speak to you am
he."

Part III

The Path of Wisdom

18

The Eclipse of Doctrine

All four of my wife's grandparents migrated to America from Greece. Chryse grew up in the Orthodox Church and attended a Greek school, and our courtship was in many ways remarkably like that portrayed in the film *My Big Fat Greek Wedding*. The more bizarre it gets, the more it resembles our story, until it seems like a documentary made without our blessing.

Despite all this, my wife had never visited Greece until our 25th wedding anniversary. We spent the majority of the trip on three islands in the Aegean: Naxos, Ikarea, and Patmos, each smaller than the last. We had almost a week on Patmos, the tiny speck of land where the apostle John was exiled and where he had the visions that have come down to us as the Book of Revelation. The Orthodox have built a monastery on the site of the cave where they think John had the apocalyptic dreams that have haunted humankind ever since. Today, the cruise ships disgorge their boluses of tourists onto the little wharf, and the buses and taxis then grind up the hill to the cave and the stalls of cheap icons.

All good things in this life end, and we had to return to England, children, and other responsibilities. On our last night on Patmos, we had to leave our hotel early to wait for the big, empty ferry that arrived at midnight to take us back to the world of airports and parking lots. As we stood on the quay, it drizzled miserably. The change in weather reflected our mood.

Very late, we both looked up into the sky at the same moment, just as a break in the clouds opened overhead, and what we saw—given where we were—made our hearts jump: a blood-red full moon. It wasn't, on this occasion, a harbinger of the end of history. It was a total lunar eclipse. We hadn't heard about this on our travels, and so it caught us by surprise—and appeared to us already complete.

For me, the strange thing about a lunar eclipse is that the shadow passing over the distant surface of the moon is our own. As I consider the New Story and its suspicions and our common-sense theology, I think I see a similar shadow over Christian doctrine. Perhaps there is a story to be told about the gradual advance of this shadow, but to my eyes the eclipse looks already complete. And, as with the moon, the shadow cast is our own.

In conversation with students, the complaints I hear most often against Christian doctrine are threefold. Some tell me that doctrine feels irrelevant to them. Its answers don't fit their questions, or meet their needs, or alleviate their pain. Others say that Christian doctrine is now impossible to believe. The "hard" sciences and the social sciences have all moved on, and so have our ethics. Others again say that the history of Christian doctrine is tragic, a story of intolerance, hatred, division, and persecution. This triple shadow is deep.

I have already said a little about the attempts we make to reduce the shadow. We form new doctrines that don't feel old, or attempt to discover deeper meanings behind or beneath the old ones. Books and films about Jesus often do the latter. In the next-to-last chapter in most books about Jesus the authors have to deal with the Resurrection, and it is common for them to assume that we simply cannot believe Jesus rose from the dead as his earliest followers claimed. Nonetheless, they show that this doesn't make the doctrine of the Resurrection untenable or unimportant—there's a deeper meaning behind or beneath the Old Story.

The strongest response to the shadow, however, is to abandon doctrine as the thing that is supposed to unite us. If doctrine loses this integrating role, there can be peace between Christians. They'll no longer ask each other if they believe the right things, and they won't condemn each other as innovators or heretics or unorthodox. If doctrine loses this role, there can be peace between the different religions. At the beginning of the twenty-first century, such a peace seems important. In the past century, much of the violence that scarred the world was over ideology: fascism versus communism versus democratic capitalism. But today it looks as if it may again be the turn of religion to be the cause of violence. If doctrine is no longer what is supposed to unite us, there may even be peace between people who are religious and those who are not—and then humankind could get serious about the real enemies of our species: poverty, disease, injustice, and global warming.

If we abandon doctrine as the thing that is supposed to integrate our lives as individuals and as communities, that sets our common goals and determines the hope we share, the place where we meet together and from which we set out to accomplish change, what shall we put in its stead? There are a few candidates vying for the position. We could unite around common experience. In the church, for example, we could replace the question, "What do you think is true doctrine about the Holy Spirit?" to, "Have you spoken in tongues?"

We could unite around our common longings. Whatever we believe about God, everyone wants to cope with the reality of this dying, cooling world. We yearn for meaning and purpose. We want our lives to be significant. We all want our children to be happy and safe.

Common experience or common longings sound like an improvement on doctrine as the place where we meet and from which we act. But we shall find that doctrine sneaks in among the ideals unbidden.

The shadow that has fallen across doctrine is much wider. Doctrines are ideas, and a great many of us have a significant distrust of ideas. We are, for the most part, not interested in abstractions, and in fact we're suspicious of them. We think they are smoke and mirrors that deceive us and keep us from seeing clearly. We like to keep an ironic distance between us and our ideas. If I don't commit myself to an abstraction, I can't be disappointed by it, and I'm free to deconstruct it. If I'm not committed to it, an idea can make no rightful demands on me. I'm not obligated. And because we take this attitude, in the few cases where we *do* make a commitment we feel that if anyone attacks our ideas they're attacking us. Any disagreement over an idea becomes a concern over giving offense and being arrogant, and we are very anxious not to be seen as intolerant.

Let me give an example of the larger dimensions of the shadow. We have lunchtime discussions at the community I live in. At one lunch, someone may begin talking about homosexuality as the others embark on their pasta. This first speaker is a Christian and he denounces a homosexual lifestyle as immoral. The reasons he gives may or may not be derived from Scripture and may or may not carry weight with those who don't attach any authority to the Bible or believe that the God it portrays has a right to make moral demands of us.

Often, a second person at the table will then ask the first, "Have you ever had any gay friends?" If the first person has to admit that he hasn't, you can at once feel the force drain out of the arguments he has just deployed.

Almost as often, there is a third person at the table who is a modifier, a peace-maker. This person says that she, too, used to disapprove of homosexuality—maybe for similar reasons—until, that is, she made friends with a gay person or couple. Now she can no longer be condemning. She doesn't feel any inclination to be gay herself, but she no longer thinks it's wrong for others.

The subject doesn't have to be sexuality—it could just as easily be Buddhism or almost anything else. Three different voices are heard: first, an exposition of ideas, then an appeal to experience acquired in relationship, and finally, a tale of ideas being modified by relationship.

It has helped me to see what may have always been obvious to everyone else: we are relational, and our relationships affect what we think is right or wrong or true or false.

19

Ethos versus Doctrine

A man studied with our community for two terms—that is, the better part of six months. He almost never spoke at any of the dozens of lunchtime discussions we had in this time, but listened for hours and hours without contributing. So, when one day he spoke up, we paid attention with eager curiosity.

What he said came out not in a torrent of words, maybe, but certainly in a steady stream. This is the gist of it:

> True ideas may exist about morality and spirituality. They may exist, but we can't be sure about any of them.
>
> If we could be certain about any such ideas, then everyone would agree. But obviously we believe different things about morality and spirituality.
>
> Because we can't be sure about ideas, we become pragmatic instead. What is important for

us about an idea is not whether it is true or
false but whether it works—and by "works" we
mean "gives us meaning and happiness."

And because we can't be sure about ideas, we
take refuge in relationships. If you can't be sure
that you're right, don't place your weight on
ideas, but get to know people instead. Ideas
don't work because they get in the way of relationships, because we can't agree with each
other. After all, when did an idea ever bring me
happiness? But friendships help me all the time
to find meaning and happiness.

At this point, someone else at the table who valued doctrine
asked him how he could live this way, doubting that his ideas
were true.

Being wrong in your ideas is not such a bad
thing [he replied, smiling]. You get used to it.
Relationships are more important than ideas,
and emotions are more reliable than reason to
get me what I want. Because we are uncertain,
we are pragmatic, and because we learn to prefer good relationships to right ideas, having the
right ethos, or tone of voice, is more important
than what you say.

We can be sure about ethos even when we can't
be sure about our ideas. We can tell that our
ethos is right because it helps our relationships
to flourish. We can find agreement with one

> another in ethos even when we can't find agree-
> ment in ideas.[1]

I began noticing this word "ethos" a couple of years ago. One context in which I heard it was in the denomination to which my church belongs. This denomination places a high value on doctrine as the focus of unity, and together we subscribe to a lengthy "confession of faith," written several centuries ago. We are a small group of churches, isolated amidst the secular culture of Europe and its indifference to our doctrines. However, we were encouraged when another small denomination that subscribed to the same confession of faith approached us with a proposal to become officially united.

As they said, when our doctrine is identical, unity is a duty. What could keep us apart? But as my colleagues discussed the matter, we decided against the proposal. Our principal reason was that, although we agreed in our doctrine, there was a major difference in our ethos. We could wish each other well and co-operate in various activities, but we didn't want to be joined if it meant that we were responsible for their ethos.

The concept, however important, is very difficult to nail down. For my purposes, ethos is the prevalent tone or sentiment of a people or a community, whereas doctrine is a body of teaching—a system of ideas considered true and important. Part of an ethos is the tone of voice in which we express our doctrines.

We can attempt to replace doctrine with ethos as the focus of unity and integration. Contemporary common-sense theology

---

1. I don't think that every question in this cascade necessarily "follows" the question that precedes it, but many people seem to find the sequence familiar and persuasive.

prefers to pay attention to ethos, which it finds more rewarding than doctrine because it is concerned for relationships. Ethos is not divorced from the way we relate to others as doctrine can be. Relationships are never irrelevant to our happiness, we don't outgrow our need of them—and good relationships would do away with most of the horrible history that an emphasis on doctrine has generated. This is why in our common-sense theology today our ethos, our tone of voice, can be more precious to us than our ideas.

I both agree and disagree with this strategy of replacing doctrine with ethos. Let me explain why. When we focus on doctrine, we imply that the key to religion is knowing the right things, assenting to the right abstract propositions. We indicate that the goal of theology is knowledge. But I don't think this is true, and I don't think this is what the Bible teaches. The prophets and the apostles do place great emphasis on knowing what is true about ourselves and about God, but they don't teach that the goal of theology is knowledge or that the key to religion is knowing the right things. The notion that propositions can be true and can be known as true and that human language can bear the weight of divine revelation is critical for Christianity. This is not the same as agreeing that the goal of theology is knowledge and the key to religion is knowing the right things.

It is useful to ask, when you're engaged in any activity, how you will know when you are succeeding. To take an example, in an earlier chapter I said that we have succeeded in answering someone's question, "Why *should* I do such and such?" when we have shown that the request was inspired by love. Any imperative to do something should be grounded in love of neighbor, love of self, love of God. When we succeed in answering that kind of question, it means we have arrived at love—even if other parties involved can't quite see it.

Of course, we can answer a question without persuading other people, just as I can solve a math problem in my eight-year-old daughter's homework even if she doesn't follow my steps. In fact, this is what is most frustrating about doing the math homework of someone you love. It has been decades since you thought about how you actually know that these are the right steps, and you forget what makes it difficult to follow them. You find it hard to explain—and yet you've arrived at the answer in the back of the book.

Before we can claim to have been thoroughly successful in persuading someone who has questioned an imperative, she needs to have seen that it's inspired by love and be satisfied that she ought to obey it. Just as with the math homework, she needs to understand the steps we have taken and be able to work out a similar problem herself. When we speak about God and His reasons for giving us a particular moral command, we may answer the question—and answer it well enough—and yet still not persuade the other person. We can't be satisfied unless she *is* persuaded and can recognize God's love in His command, and yet there are many reasons beyond our control, and beyond simple reasoning, why that love sometimes goes unrecognized. In other words, Christians can respond to the New Story but it is almost certain that not everyone will be persuaded by the response.

What, then, counts for success in theology if not knowledge of the truth? I shall try to answer this a bit more thoroughly later, but for now let me suggest that success in theology is related to success in life. It's not an academic pursuit that doesn't touch our lives. It's not a word game for people interested in that sort of thing, which others can ignore without missing anything. We all do our theology, even those of us who claim to be agnostic or insist that we're just not interested.

Not everyone will accept this immediately. After all, to many of us, theology seems irrelevant. We do not need a theologian in the same way we need a dentist. Theology does not stand over us with power in the same way a dentist may stand over us, her drill poised. Yet we do need theology.

The goal of theology is not knowledge but wisdom.

Wisdom is the integration of knowledge and emotion and behavior with the reality of life in the universe in which we find ourselves. One theologian has called it "performance knowledge."[2] This is helpful because it sees that wisdom incorporates knowledge but includes more than knowledge, and it makes demands of us that knowledge alone does not make.

When the British managed to break the German naval codes in the Second World War, the Admiralty was not satisfied with mere knowledge. It would have been foolish to say, "There! We've done the task assigned us. We've broken their codes." Knowledge of what the U-boat commanders were radioing back to their superiors was turned into wisdom when the Admiralty acted on that knowledge and redirected the convoys sailing across the Atlantic. Most of the people involved in that secret work at Bletchley Park during the war had never seen a U-boat or had a torpedo launched at them, but what would we think of those geniuses and their remarkable efforts if the knowledge they discovered had never changed the course of a single ship?

---

2. Kevin Vanhoozer in his two books *Is There a Meaning in This Text?* and *First Theology.*

We can study theology and discuss it as if the remarkable feat of breaking the code is enough—attending to detail, seeing the patterns, learning the esoteric language, knowing the truth. The Bible, however, teaches that such theology is vanity.

Wisdom is performance knowledge, but I believe that it draws a larger circle than even knowledge and the actions that arise from knowledge. Here our language fails us because (so far as I know) we don't have a verb that conveys all that being wise involves—a word that incorporates "think," "feel," and "do." Wisdom embraces true knowledge about the world and right action prompted by that knowledge—and further, the appropriate emotional response to both.

The British code-breakers discovered what the U-boats were up to and as a result the Admiralty changed the courses of the convoys, though not so much or so often that the Germans realized that their codes had been broken. There would have been something wrong with a code-breaker or a naval planner who was disappointed with or depressed about the outcome of his knowledge and his actions. If any of them had stood on the quay watching a convoy safely entering port and had felt no sense of joy and relief and achievement, we wouldn't consider him wise. Such emotions should accompany his knowledge and the actions that arise from it. We can, of course, consider them separately, but wisdom integrates knowledge, action, and emotion.

To know that a god exists, and what kind of god it is, is a penultimate goal of the human enterprise we call "theology." The God who exists has the rights of a creator and the moral authority of an infallible judge, and He is the ground of ethics. Accordingly, theology ought to lead us to change our courses as we discover our meaning, purpose, and significance in relation to Him. But there are also emotions that are appropriate to the discovery of human significance in a God who wants to be reconciled with His creatures, to solve the problem of the sacred, and to be the source of hope for a better future by destroying evil, and who has rights over us not merely because He exists but because He has earned them by stripping Himself of all His privileges and dwelling among us. It would be foolish to feel happy and satisfied without accepting that reconciliation, still living under the danger of that impartial judgment. It would be foolish not to allow that reconciliation and that hope of the coming Kingdom to bring joy—even though we must also be for the moment, as the Christ was, "acquainted with grief."

Of course, there are things that obstruct the integration of our emotions with our knowledge and our actions. Some Christians do despair, even though their birthright is hope. It is possible to know something and not integrate it with our behavior. In Graham Greene's book *The Heart of the Matter*, a Catholic police officer is having an affair with a woman who doesn't believe in God. At one point she says to him that he cannot believe in God either, because if he did he wouldn't sneak out of his house to be with her. The unbelieving mind tells itself that if it did believe it would integrate that knowledge into its behavior. But the policeman replies, quite rightly, that he does believe but he still comes to be with her. We don't always live according to our moral knowledge.

There are things that obstruct the integration of our emotions with our actions—we must not be simplistic or we may crush ourselves beneath new burdens of guilt. It seems to me that what is important is never to accept as normal a situation in which our knowledge, actions, and emotions do not agree. We can, of course, find that we are dis-integrated, but we mustn't think that this is the best we can hope for, that there isn't a better future. And, as I have said earlier, Christianity doesn't see ignorance or even disobedience as the ultimate problem. The source of the deepest dis-integration is distrust. The just shall live by faith.

There are obstructions to integration, and it is not a one-way flow from thinking to feeling to acting. These three elements influence one another in a very complex way. Certain kinds of modern thought would claim that reason is dispassionate, unrelated to, and abstracted from character and behavior. This story can be told historically. The Enlightenment might claim that the process of knowing is crucial. That emphasis is understandable—after all, the scientific method was proving to be such a powerful way of discovering knowledge and making human beings successful agents of change in the world. Understandably, people became obsessed with getting the process right, and thought that the right process would ensure that we could arrive at the truth apart from traditions and authorities that had their own, self-interested agendas. We could trust only reason to be disinterested. Reason alone was the path to truth and to human flourishing. It alone could lead us to the better future.

However, the process became too powerful and formed an agenda of its own. The way the Enlightenment obtained knowledge had some limitations—places it couldn't go and questions it couldn't answer—but rather than acknowledging them, some thinkers insisted that everything beyond these limits was irrational. If it couldn't answer a particular question, it dismissed it as not a genuine question, which could therefore be ignored. This new tyranny of thought insisted that the answers to all genuine questions can be discovered and the means of discovering them can be taught to others. It also affirmed that all answers to genuine questions must be compatible with each other.[3]

The first reaction against the Enlightenment and the tyranny of the new method was not the Postmodernism of the late twentieth century but the Romanticism of the early eighteenth, which rebelled not against knowledge but against any method that insisted on ruling out questions of meaning, purpose, and value that seemed important for humankind to answer.

I have told a very large story very briefly, but the point is this: increasingly, we realize that the way in which we know things—our epistemology, to use the technical word—is influenced and enabled by things the Enlightenment might have thought of as ethics, and therefore as uncertain and unjustified. Our emotions and our behavior influence what we know. It is not a simple matter of knowledge leading to action. We have to be involved, and virtuously so, in order to grow in knowledge. In a clumsy example, it would be possible for a dishonest, untrustworthy man at the Admiralty to assume, not unreasonably, that German U-boat commanders were as unreliable as he, and not to believe a word of their decoded messages, not to act on any of the information, to stand on the quay, and feel no sorrow when a merchant ship failed to arrive.

However, wisdom is not threatened by this requirement that we be virtuous knowers, that we don't cheat or deceive ourselves. Likewise, Christianity doesn't need to fear this demand, for just as God is the ground of being and the ground of ethics, so also

---

3. See Isaiah Berlin's *The Roots of Romanticism* for an account of what he calls the "rationalist Western tradition."

He is the ground of knowing. Wisdom's agenda doesn't rule out questions because they do not fit into a single, all-embracing process. Knowledge isn't everything. The Bible teaches that doctrine isn't everything. It insists that the demons know the doctrine about God better than we do,[4] but although they're smart, they're not wise.

Truth does matter to wisdom—it is best to be integrated into the world as it is. We want to be integrated emotionally into reality—it is dying and decaying. We will feel and behave differently amidst the frustration of the universe if we know that the good is going to outlast the evil. It matters for a better hope if the Kingdom does actually arrive with judgment and then a consummation of celebration. Wisdom wants to know the truth. Will there be a judgment? Will a Kingdom of God break into our experience? And yet wisdom is not satisfied with a knowledge of the truth alone. It insists that a belief in the Kingdom must be "performance knowledge"—it must influence our decisions and our actions.[5]

If the story the Bible tells is true, then wisdom is the integration of my knowledge, my emotions, and my behavior with this Creator, this fall, this curse of all things, this hope of redemption, this judgment, and this promise of a coming Kingdom. Christians are not wise when they integrate only part

---

4. James 2:19.

5.   This is why it's wrong to ask anyone to deny her religion, or indeed any worldview, in the public arena, as if she could exclude it from the secular business of public life. As T. S. Eliot would have it, "The compulsion to live in such a way that Christian behavior is only possible in a restricted number of situations, is a very powerful force against Christianity; for behavior is as potent to affect belief as belief to affect behavior." I would add only that any theology could be substituted for "Christianity" in this observation.

of the story—having room, say, for lamentation or joy but not both. And someone who is not a Christian, if she is wise, is in some degree integrated into parts of this true story, even if she doesn't accept all of it. We shouldn't be surprised that a homosexual couple can be good neighbors or that a Buddhist pays his debts. Relationships with people we disagree with allow us to meet wisdom in places we may not have expected it.

In other words, the New Story is a quest for wisdom, an attempt to find the good God—but it can also be a tragic tale of folly if the goodness of God is mistaken for evil and left behind as the search moves on.

I appreciate this emphasis on ethos, as long as it is an insistence that knowledge is not enough, as long as it attempts to integrate knowledge with emotion. Ethos recognizes that emotions must not be ignored in the search for knowledge. Christianity sees the limitations of both the Enlightenment's trust in reason and Romanticism's rebellion against it. It can offer a reason both to discover and to create. Christianity can give a reason for discovering a reality that does not depend on our interpretation for its existence. It can also give a reason for creating new things within that reality that do depend upon us.

Wisdom is more integrated than ethos, because ethos is tempted to ignore knowledge. You can say very different things in a loving tone of voice. Wisdom is more integrated than ethos because it demands that behavior should be included and that we shouldn't be satisfied with words and attitudes that sound and look loving. Sometimes—in fact, oftentimes—in this world it can be very loving to tell someone that he's wrong. It isn't always an attack.

Christians do not need to modify their doctrine and theology so much as to rediscover the Bible's message of wisdom. Those who insist that the Bible is true should demonstrate the integration of knowledge, emotion, and behavior. Wisdom always knows, feels, and acts *in its day*—it doesn't live in the past; neither does it throw out the past.

Wisdom is fearing, loving, and obeying the God who exists. I am confident that the Christ taught the same:

> Therefore everyone who hears these words of mine and puts them into practice, is like a wise man who built his house on the rock. The rain came down, the streams rose, and the winds blew and beat against that house; yet it did not fall, because it had its foundation on the rock.

> But everyone who hears these words of mine and does not put them into practice is like a foolish man who built his house on sand. The rain came down, the streams rose, and the winds blew and beat against that house, and it fell with a great crash.[6]

---

6. Matthew 7:24–27.

20

Where to Begin?

The goal of theology is wisdom, and we measure our progress toward it by how successful we are at living. Whatever theologizing we do, we should set a course for these. Theology is never merely academic in nature, never satisfied with just accumulating knowledge. But where should we start our theology if we are not simply going to be diverted into contemporary common-sense ideas? What do we need by way of introduction? What do we have to know before we begin to learn? Does the choice of a starting point determine where we end up?

The question of where to begin is a really difficult one. The answer is not obvious—or, rather, different answers seem obvious to different people. Should we begin with ourselves when we do theology, begin with our reason, our experience, and then argue outwards towards God, or spiritual reality? Or should we begin with a community and its traditions? Or should we begin with divine revelation and allow some word from God to tell us

about ourselves, our reason, our experience and our community
and its traditions?

Anyone familiar with the common stereotypes of John
Calvin might expect him to insist that we must begin with God
and His revelation. And yet that great advocate of the importance of the Bible opens his most famous work by saying that the
starting-point is not obvious:

> Nearly all the wisdom we possess, that is to say,
> true and sound wisdom, consists of two parts:
> the knowledge of God and of ourselves. But,
> while joined by many bonds, which one pre-
> cedes and brings forth the other is not easy to
> discern.[1]

Let me stress that theology is not "theologian-ology." We
may learn from other people, their reason and experience, their
community and traditions, their interpretation of divine revelation. Nevertheless, unlike so much academic effort, theology
is not primarily a matter of mastering the opinions of various
prominent thinkers. It isn't a matter of showing how comfort-
ably one can navigate a bibliography. Its true and distant goal is
always wisdom and success in life.[2]

I live in a community where people come to stay for a while
to ask questions about metaphysics, epistemology, ethics, lan-

---

1. *Institutes of the Christian Religion.*

2. "Success in life" here does not mean financial security or comfort in our
private circumstances. Rather, it means discovery of a better hope: that which
is good, helps us flourish in the present and finally proves to be true. I would
suggest that it is also connected, as Jesus taught, with love of God, love of
neighbor, and love of self.

guage, and aesthetics. Sometimes when I am giving a tutorial I start to open the Bible on the table by my armchair and, for any one of a host of reasons, the student gets angry and says, "Don't open that book!" I'm always interested to discover in due course why he reacted so strongly, but I do close the book. I think I can address his question without recourse to the Bible. I could turn to the window in my office that looks out on a garden and a patch of sky and a beautiful brick wall and we could begin with the world we inhabit. Or I could sit back in my chair and ask him about the story of his life and what it feels like to be him. I could share my story and how I find it being me. Or instead I could turn to the bookshelves that line my wall: perhaps my student is happy to read, he just doesn't wish to read the Bible. It's silly to try to find out what God is like and yet not be curious about what He has revealed of Himself to others. I can sympathize with an enquirer who wonders, "Why must we begin with *that* particular book?"

A unitary reality and an integrated wisdom invite us to learn from the Bible and the view from my window, from my story, and the stories of others. Each of these modes of revelation has its virtues, but also its limitations and its dangers.

I would urge us to begin our theology with a desire: we should want to discover what to thank and who to worship. When we want to know these, our theology will always range further than our small selves. We can look within ourselves for many things, but never for what to thank or who to worship. This is not a quest for the indifferent nor for the uncommitted, as broken dreams will have to be faced. In an earlier chapter I have suggested the importance of gratitude as a human virtue and the part our ingratitude plays in distancing God from us.

The way the Bible puts it is this, "Anyone who comes to Him must believe that He exists and that He rewards those who earnestly seek Him."[3] This doesn't mean we must have our minds made up before we begin, but it does mean that certain kinds of pessimism and cynicism can keep our eyes closed and prevent us from seeing the very thing we say we want to find.

Could the aim of our theology instead be to try to discover what to blame and who to curse? I think there are two reasons why the answer is no. Identifying the good seems to be more powerful than identifying the bad in a world of frustration and decay. The bad can evidently take so many forms, and the good can deteriorate and distort in so many ways. I suspect that there are many more false trails than true ones, and many more counterfeits than actualities. I could search for a wife by beginning with the whole of womankind and then ruling out, one by one, all the women I *wouldn't* want to spend the rest of my days with; but it doesn't seem the likeliest way to find what I'm looking for.

It is possible we may find that nothing is good, there is nothing to thank—only the blind necessity of cause-and-effect. It is possible we may conclude that there is no one to worship. Of course, I think that would be a mistake, which would lead to tragedy and despair. But even if we arrived at such terrible conclusions, I think it would still be healthier to look for something to be grateful to and someone to worship, which would more likely lead to successful living.

My second reason to prefer a positive theology to a negative one is that it seems less likely that we will get lost in an internal

---

3. Hebrews 11:6.

maze, stuck in ourselves, never to emerge again. If we seek to blame and curse we may never escape from our own egos, and we will find that some (though not all) of the fault lies inside us.

We should begin our theology where we are—but not stay where we are.

Even if you don't know where to begin your speech, you cannot go on clearing your throat forever. The most important thing about theology is not being certain of your starting place but knowing your goal. This is because theology is a dance between multiple poles. It is a great circle, and you can break into it at several different places.

"Do I begin my theology with me or with a community of other people?" Begin where you are, but don't stay where you are.

If you are used to quoting the beliefs of your family or the teachings of your tradition or the opinions of the media, progress to examining them critically in the light of your reason and of revelation. We have to question even our own community— but if you have wandered too far away to hear what they have discovered about what to thank and who to worship, go and listen to them again.

We also need to expose God's revelation to ideas from other sources. For example, we are right to be shocked when the biblical witnesses tell us that Jesus rose from the dead. We feel shock because we come to the Bible knowing that dead things do not come back to life.[4] Our science tells us this. Even if we had

---

4. We don't have to make the mistake of David Hume, however, and say that this miracle is so overwhelmingly improbable that *any* other explanation for the testimony of Scripture is more likely to be true.

decided to begin with the Bible, it's clear that we have already
started elsewhere. The biblical witnesses were shocked by what
they saw, and I would suggest that they intend us to be shocked
by their claim—rather than simply swallowing it because we
have "begun with the Bible" or with a tradition that has learned
to accept the Resurrection.

Begin your theology where you are, but don't stay where
you are.

Begin with a sense of shock at what the Bible reports, because dead people don't come back to life, but allow the revelation to correct you. You are right that dead people don't come
back to life—but on this occasion someone did.

If we begin with our community and stay within its tradition, this will diminish the awe the Resurrection properly
evokes. We shall have a weaker grasp of what to thank and who
to worship. We could believe in the Resurrection and yet be
stuck in a small world that does not touch the reality outside.
Beginning with our community and staying there doesn't help
us to integrate our knowledge with our emotions and our behavior. We know that dead people don't come back to life, and
are shocked at the suggestion—but on this occasion someone
did come back, and as a result we can experience the hope that
death and decay may not be as final as life and light. And, rec-
ognizing that this life is not all we should take into account
when we decide how to spend our treasure and our time, we can
behave accordingly.

"Do I begin with reason or with revelation?" Begin where
you are, but don't stay where you are.

If you know Scripture well, let it begin to converse with
your reason. On the other hand, if you have long been locked

up in the small closet of your own thoughts and values, let the revelation of the prophets and the apostles wrest open the door and let some light and fresh air in.

"Do I begin with my particular experience or with some universal truth?" Begin where you are, but don't stay where you are.

If you have coped with pain and disappointment by repeating religious clichés and denying what has happened to you in this dark world, I would say, go and take your experience seriously. If, on the other hand, you have been shut up in that pain and disappointment looking (when you bother to look) for something to blame and someone to curse, I would say, escape from your experiences by listening to some voices from outside. Read Revelation and what it has to say about your experience. Discover that the Creator is angry at evil and has suffered Himself in order to put an end to suffering. Be open to the wisdom of the community that knows the Christ who emptied himself and thus earned his authority.

Each of us is already somewhere on the great circle, even those of us who don't believe in any god or don't feel a need for one. The Bible describes God as worth seeking and says that He can respond to our searching around the great circle. The path of wisdom leads to the better hope that each of us needs.